Scars

Leaving Pain In The Past

By

Keith Edmonds

Dedication

I dedicate this book to you.

To you, the one holding it in your hands; the one reading my words. Maybe you have picked it up because you also have scars. Don't we all? My hope for you is that whatever you have faced or are facing, that you will come through it better, not just changed! And with the knowledge that scars are *not* what defines us: they are just a part of the telling of the story.

And to my mother, Brenda.

What happened to me – to us – was a blessing from God. Our story started on September 9, 1977, changed forever on November 18, 1978, and is stronger today because we made it through. I hope you find comfort in knowing "the rest of the story." I love you.

Foreword

By Pamela Walker
Assistant Principal
The Academy

*"We cannot always build the future for our youth,
but we can build our youth for the future."*

~ Franklin D. Roosevelt

Located in Lebanon, Tennessee, The Academy is the alternative learning program for students in grades 6-12 in Wilson County. Students who attend school there are still enrolled in their school of record and are placed at The Academy until they earn the number of points that have been assigned to them by the SDHA (Student Discipline Hearing Authority), as a consequence of their actions.

Keith Edmonds has been coming to The Academy as long as I've worked here. At first, I wasn't sure what he did, other than show up, day after day. After watching and listening for some time, I have a much better understanding of what it is Keith does here.

First, he's a volunteer. He comes here daily because he chooses to do so. He does some substitute teaching, which has opened the door for him to see the students in a different light than when he comes to do group or meet with them. Keith comes because he loves our children. He loves the underdog who doesn't have anyone in his or her corner. Our kids are underdogs. Keith is in their corner.

Keith's not playing around. He's as real as real gets. He has a great BS meter, which means he can see and hear through what the kids do, say, and how they act, to see what's real and what isn't. He's willing to help anyone, but the kids have to first, want it, and second, be active partners in the work he does. He's taught me that we can't want success more for our students than they want it for themselves. His tolerance is low for lying and manipulation, as it has to be for all of us who engage in working with at-risk teens.

Keith is an honest story teller. He relates to our students by sharing his story, which is, quite literally, written all over his face. He shares his life story and experiences in an open and honest way, so the kids understand what he's been through in a great deal of his life. Many of our students can relate to being mistreated, abused, feeling unwanted, etc.

Because Keith has scars on his face, our students can see that his is a real story, not made-up, not embellished. He's a living testament to what happened to him, and to the fact that he's a successful and happy person on the other side of the tragedy that was his young life. Having overcome addiction and living in recovery also provides Keith a platform with our students, many of whom are dealing with additional issues and the problems that come with them, personally and in a family environment.

Keith has a genuine heart for troubled young people because he was one. He comes to The Academy daily, and is a sharing, caring volunteer, who relates to our students in a very real way by telling his story of abuse, trauma, addiction, recovery, and doing life on life's terms. He is a group leader, a speaker, a discussion facilitator, a one-on-one counselor, a teacher, a mentor, and ultimately, a friend to our students. The best thing about Keith is that our students trust him, and building trust with our kids is not an easy task.

Keith is able to build that trust because of the code by which he lives his life, and which he shares with our students every day. Keith's code is actually, C.O.D.E., an acronym that stands for the four values that guide his life: Courage, Optimism, Determination, and Encouragement. In the pages that follow he will share with you, his readers, how these four words have guided his life, even when he wasn't aware that he even had a code. You will read how these values have taken him from an abused and broken childhood to a life of sobriety and service. I hope that as you read Keith's story, you will be impacted and encouraged, just as all of us at The Academy are every day, and will find ways to apply the CODE in your own life.

Table of Contents

Introduction
Between The Truth And
A Lie

"The most confused we ever get is when we try to convince our heads of something that our hearts know is a lie"

~ Karen Marie Moning

I was drinking when I quit drinking. I was coming off a five-day bender. Each day, I'd drink until I couldn't see straight. I'd drink to the point where I'd be numb. I had no feeling and the stares from the world would fade into the darkness of my next black-out.

This Sunday was different than most. It was my 35th birthday, and I woke up with the pain and confusion from the aftermath of checking out for a couple of days. When life got too heavy for me to deal with, I'd "check out," allowing me to avoid living life on life's terms. I'd find a dark bar, a hole in the wall, and sit by myself and start casually drinking. I'd tell myself: "*I'm only going to have a couple of beers.*"

Sitting there, I'd think about the many people throughout the course of my day whom I'd see staring at the scars on my face. In public, I'd handle it with a smile, acting like it didn't affect me. I was strong, and I could handle both my facial scars and the emotional scars I've carried for so many years.

As the time passed, the anger would grow stronger – the hurt would grow stronger. The confusion surrounding why a man would hurt a baby, coming so close to killing that baby, simply for crying, allowed the anger and hurt to turn to rage. Those "couple of beers" quickly became shots of liquor, followed by more beer, followed by more shots, until I reached the numb, checked-out feeling that would allow me to put all of those emotions into the darkness where I thought they belonged – hidden away, so I wouldn't show weakness. From the beginning of my life, I had to be strong.

The night before had been a celebration of my 35th birthday. As a drunk, I loved a celebration – didn't matter the occasion – but my birthday was a time to kick it up a notch. I woke up from another blackout with not a clue of what the night before had been like. I did know there was a constant theme each time I blacked out. I'd hurt someone, or I'd end up in jail. Luckily, I only ended up in jail a few times, but each and every time I blacked out, I'd hurt someone emotionally. I wanted whoever it was to feel the pain I felt, which led me to drinking so hard. I didn't care who it was – a loved one, a good friend, a girlfriend. No one was safe from the lashing and destruction I wanted to get out.

The hangover that day was the same as every day, so I woke up, staggered to my car half dressed, the smell of booze lingering on me, and drove to a nearby gas station. I bought a beef jerky stick and three 22-ounce cans of beer. As I walked out of the store and got to my car, I opened the jerky stick and popped open a can. I needed the pain to go away and this was my normal method, drink again until the pain went away. I was constantly running from pain. I drove back to my apartment.

Once I got there, I knew I didn't want to go in, because my roommate would be there, and the last thing I wanted was conversation. What I wanted was to be alone and process my guilt and shame, and get rid of the pain that was almost crippling. I pulled into a secluded parking spot, allowing me to check out again. I sat in my car listening to music, and cracked another can open. As I'd listen to the music, I'd wonder why no one understood my need to check out.

Didn't they know the way I felt on the inside? I was going through this life getting beaten up every day. The years of stares, being called names, and dealing with the emotional warfare gave me the right to be this way. There was no saving grace for me, there was no one who could understand what I was feeling, and there was no one who understood that I was tired of living this way.

As I was sitting there, I started questioning the purpose of my life. Why am I even here? Why did something so horrific happen to me? If there *is* a God, why would this happen to me? As I opened the third beer, I took a look at my life, where it was, where it was going, and where I wanted it to be.

I was a drunk, who ran from all my problems. I couldn't hold a job for an extended period of time, and I was always behind on every bill. My credit was in shambles from years of self-destruction.

I knew if I chose to continue down this path, I was going to end up in prison from having killed or seriously injured someone or some family because of my drinking and driving. I'd drink and drive each night, not knowing what path I took home. All I was concerned about was me, not the effects of my actions on others. Or I was going to end up dead. When I thought about or looked at myself, I never liked what I saw.

I knew where I wanted my life to be. I wanted to be a mature adult who had his life together, like so many of my friends. I wanted to be happy; I wanted to smile so brightly the world would know I was happy.

I never really had a relationship with God. I honestly didn't know if he existed, and if he did, I was angry with him. Why would God allow me to go through that pain as a baby? How could he allow a man to hurt me so badly? The pain I went through as a young kid, the pain of being a teenager, and the pain of being this adult who looks so different than so many others? I had nowhere else to look to get this pain, guilt, shame, and hurt to go away.

So as I sat there in my car, listening to music, drinking what would be my last Coors Light ever, trying to go to that place of checking out, I said out loud to a God I wasn't even sure I believed would hear or help me, "God, I'm not sure if you're there, I'm not sure that it's even okay that I'm reaching out to you, but if you can hear me, I need help. I can't do this anymore. I'm tired, and I'm pissed off, and I'm really tired of being this shitty person. If you're really there, please help me. I'll do whatever it is you ask of me, if you can just please help me."

I didn't get an answer that day, but what I did get was the power to pour what was left of that third beer onto the ground. I walked into my apartment, and when my roommate asked me what I'd been doing sitting out in my car for so many hours, I said very little, went to my room and spent the rest of my 35th birthday alone.

Chapter 1
A Cruel Awakening

"Where does discipline end? Where does cruelty begin? Somewhere between these, thousands of children inhabit a voiceless hell."

~ François Mauriac

❝ ❝Why would you want a picture of THAT?" I was four years old, sitting at a Kmart photo gallery in my best new clothes, smiling as brightly and as proudly as I could while getting my picture taken, when I first discovered I was different. My mother started crying and fighting with the girl who said those hateful words. I asked her what was wrong and why she was so mad. She collected herself and told me something I, for the first time, would understand.

She told me I had scars on my face from a mean man who had hurt me. I had, as every other young child would, so many questions: Why would he want to hurt me? What did I do that was so wrong? She told me I was going to be okay, that I could be anything I wanted to be, and that he was sent to prison for hurting me so badly. That was the first time I realized I was different, and the first time I asked questions, but certainly not the last.

It began on the night of November 18, 1978, a night that plays over and over again in my head; each and every year it comes around. It was a night when I wish I could have fought back, a night I wish I could have changed, a night I wish I hadn't been crying. The man I was entrusted to – my mother's boyfriend, had done something terrible to me that would change my life forever. That night I'd become a victim and a survivor of child abuse.

Statistics show that most children who become victims of child abuse are 18 months old or younger; I was 14 months old. Statistics also show that most perpetrators are between the ages of 20 and 29; my abuser was 25. On that cold, Michigan winter night, my experience matched those statistics.

The next morning, my mother awoke to find her baby boy swollen and clinging to life. Terrified, she immediately demanded that Allen tell her what had happened. His reply was calculated and calm: "I think it's a spider bite." After she rushed me to the hospital and into the ER, the check-in nurse asked my mother what the problem was. My mother lifted the blanket that was protecting me from the bitter cold, revealing the third-degree burns I received to my face from this "spider bite."

The nurse rushed me to a room where doctors immediately began working on me. My mother wasn't allowed to come with me, but was taken to another room and separated from her boyfriend/my abuser, who was placed in yet another room. Questioning their involvement, they were asked how a child of 14 months could receive such traumatic burns to his face. This was no spider bite!

As I tell this part of my story, I would expect that you, the reader, is wondering where I learned these details. Much of this information came through conversations with my mother, hard conversations that we had over the years, as well as from court documents that I obtained much later in life. The story is as complete as I can tell it. I am certain that there are details which will never be known, as they exist only in the heart and mind of the man who was responsible for my abuse.

At Death's Door

Doctors and surgeons believed the abuse I received was too much for an infant to handle and that I was going to die. Of the number of children who have died from abuse or neglect, nearly eighty percent are younger than four years of age. That night, I could have easily become a statistic, as a victim of yet another violent crime against children. As I lay there clinging to life, the doctors went out to my mother and told her to say her goodbyes to her son.

It was at that point, for the first time, God's hand would pull me from the depths of death. When they spoke to my mother about the accident that caused this burn, she claimed her innocence, insisting she had nothing to do with harming her first and only child. My mother believes she was drugged and, still to this day, has no recollection of that night. Drugging her would have allowed this man to commit an inhumane act that nearly resulted in my death.

The day after the abuse, my mother came to the hospital to tell me my biological father was coming to visit me. The nurse questioned my mother, and said, "His father has been in his room, holding him all night." My mother looked through the glass window into my room and her heart nearly stopped; there I was, cradled in the arms of the man who caused all this harm. I suppose my abuser had led the hospital staff to believe he was my father. He had been left with me, all night, unattended, and was acting like he loved me. Was he there to show remorse? Was he there to cause more abuse? Was he there to kill me?

When I was examined at the hospital, it was found that I had actually been being abused for some time prior to this near fatal abuse. Cigarettes had been put out on the bottoms of my feet. While it's still unclear as to who called Child Protective Services to my mother's apartment, it was never actually determined who had burned my feet with cigarettes. My mom's boyfriend wasn't a smoker.

It was a clever move on his part. Because he wasn't a smoker, he was initially dismissed as the offender. At the hospital, after the doctors had attended to the burns on my face, they discovered that both of my legs had been broken. And, as it turned out, all of the abuse I had suffered was determined to have been caused by the man who caused my face to be so badly burned.

The case worker assigned to my mother was a kind woman named Lois, who believed in my mother's innocence right from the beginning, believed she could win the custody case, and that my mother would never lose custody of me. However, my mother told Lois she needed to stop fighting the custody case and that I'd do better, at least temporarily, in the foster care system.

My mom was a naïve, teenage mother. She was a kid raising a kid. She was just 19 years old, struggling with how to be an adult and a "mom." Now she was dealing with the guilt of allowing herself to be involved with a man who nearly took her child's life, and who had left him scarred for life. She knew she needed some help to figure out why she was able to let this happen. Parenting classes, therapy of some kind, something: she didn't know what she needed, but she was smart enough and brave enough to realize that getting me back right then wouldn't be the best thing for either of us.

Lois asked my mother if she knew anyone in the foster care system. She didn't, but one of her cousins volunteered to serve as my foster parent. So, Lois asked the judge that I be placed in her care and that my mother would have full visitation rights. The judge agreed, and I became a ward of the State of Michigan.

For my new foster mom/cousin, her offer to care for me brought unplanned and unexpected results. The role of foster parent suited her so well that it became her life work, for the benefit of the many children she'd love and care for over the years. My mom and my cousin decided that she would be referred to as my "aunt".

It was the end of January 1979 – nearly three full months since I'd been abused – when I was released from the hospital. I walked out with my mother holding one hand and my aunt holding the other. My mother gave me a hug and a kiss, said she loved me so much and that I was going to stay with my aunt for a little while, and said goodbye. After she left, I went with my aunt to what would be my temporary home.

While living with her, there was another foster child about my age named Billy, and we became playmates. It was a safe family environment for me, and my mother would visit me every day. This gave her the opportunity to observe how my aunt worked with the other foster children, and to learn parenting skills. After six months of being a ward of the State of Michigan, the day before the custody court hearing, my aunt came to my mother's apartment with adoption papers, asking her to sign away the rights to her baby. But my mother refused; she wanted me back. She wanted us to start a new life together and build a family.

When the custody court date arrived, it was late June. My mother was about to learn if she'd regain custody or not. She had made the difficult decision of placing me in foster care, knowing I deserved better than she could give me at that particular time in her life. She knew she was broken, and needed help.

She wasn't afraid of the decision she'd made to temporarily give up her parental rights, and had faith that she would eventually get me back. She got the help she needed, and was able to learn proper parenting skills from my aunt. With her heart in her throat, she listened to the judge grant her full custody. This time, when we walked out of the courthouse, she was holding me. I was reunited with my mother and we were going home, together.

After being extremely vague when he appeared in court about abusing me, and continually denying any intent to harm me, my abuser finally agreed to go into detail of that night and the abuse. This would be the third time the judge would see him. Previously, he had denied any intent to actually harm me. Court records showed that my face had been pressed up against a heat register on a wall, because I was crying and had made a mess in my diaper. I probably stopped crying when he hurt me, because according to what I have read about the body's reaction to such trauma I should have immediately gone into shock, which would have caused me to stop crying. I can't remember the pain, but I can imagine the pain I must have felt! It was the actions of that man, with intent to do great bodily harm, which would change my life forever.

He received a ten-year sentence in a state prison, while I received what I thought was a life sentence of feeling alone, alienated, and angry. Growing up a survivor of child abuse, I'd often ask myself those same questions I had asked my mother. Why did he want to hurt me? What did I do that was so wrong? I always felt alone, and my mind always went back to those same questions. That's where my loneliness began, my confusion grew, and my anger built.

An Annual Ordeal

Each year until I was 14, and then every other year, my mother and I, and sometimes other family members, would drive to the Shriners Burn Institute in Cincinnati, Ohio. This was my least favorite place on earth. When I was there, I was angry. I had multiple photos taken of my scars from every angle, and I was asked to smile while they took what felt like thousands of photos.

Why would I want to smile? I've never liked having my picture taken. When you have scars on your face, one of the last things you want is someone taking photos of you. When I looked at photos of myself, all I saw was the damage from my abuser. How was I expected to live a "normal" life with a constant reminder that I was abused for crying as an infant?

Once they'd finished taking all the photos, I'd have to go into a cold white room and wait, just my mother and me sitting in a room until the doctors arrived. I'd tell her how much I hated it, and that I didn't want to be there. Then the doctors would come in and discuss the photos with my mom, right in front of me. The words I heard were: "Ohhh, look at that," "Ouch," "Poor kid." I doubt that was what they actually said, but that is what my memory tells me I heard.

My surgeon was an older man with dark black hair; he wore glasses that fit on the tip of his nose, almost like he was looking down on me. The room was always well lit but there was a sense of tension, tension that could be matched to an interrogation room in a jail. He'd touch and stretch my scar while talking into a little recorder box and documenting everything he saw. Then came the worst part, the inevitable fitting for a new face mask.

The doctor in charge of creating the mask was a short, stocky guy who, for some reason, reminded me of Pat Sajak from *Wheel of Fortune*. To this day, I can't watch that show without seeing him running through my mind and hearing him say, "You have to stay still or we're going to have to hold you down," while I was screaming and crying because I was against having to wear a mask. I had already been abused and had scars on my face: I was already different. Why would I want to wear a mask that was painful and more degrading?

I'd have to lie flat in a cold room while they layered on paste that would form to my face, cutting out holes for my eyes, nose, and mouth. It felt like I was being buried alive. The whole time I was kicking and screaming in anger and rage at my abuser. Why do I have to go through this? What did I do that was so wrong? Why did he want to hurt me so bad?

Each and every year as I grew, I'd have to go through the same emotions and procedures to get fitted for a new mask. Each year, I built up more and more hate for my abuser. I have to say the doctor who created my mask was by far my least favorite person at the Burn Institute. The mask would make me look even more different, having it stuck to my face, pulling and stretching my scar.

This would prove to be a constant battle when we got home from my yearly checkup. My mother would try and force me to wear the mask and I'd continue to fight it. I was supposed to wear it all day, just taking it off enough to allow my skin to breathe. I'd only wear it for a little bit in the evening, then I'd take it off once she put me to bed and closed the door.

In the fall of 1987, I was ten years old and entering the fourth grade. However, that year I wasn't starting school on time. I was getting ready for the first surgery I'd remember. I went to have my nostrils enlarged. After I was abused, my nostrils shrunk from the burns, causing me to have trouble breathing. Surgeons took skin from behind my ears, placing catheters in my nostrils and allowing the skin to build up around them. Two months later the catheters were removed.

When I was 12, my mother and the surgeons began discussing the option of doing more surgeries – surgeries that would allow them to completely reconstruct my face. But I told her I didn't want any more surgeries, even though it could mean that my scars would be less noticeable. I was ready for the masks, the surgeries and the trips to be over.

With that, I started to grow into the man I am today. I accepted the fact that I'm a survivor of child abuse, and *I thought* I was ready to face this world without feeling shame or guilt for being abused. Wearing the mask became less of an issue, the surgeries finally ended, and the trips to the Burn Institute were few and far between. It was at this time that I could finally focus on trying to be a "normal" kid, which led to me becoming a "normal" adult. At least that was what I thought. Time would prove that I wasn't exactly as ready as I thought.

Chapter 2
My New Family

"Alcoholism isn't a spectator sport. Eventually the whole family gets to play."

~ Joyce Burditt

When I was four years old, my mother married a man named Jim. She was trying to build a stable life for us. Jim worked in the shop at General Motors and my mother worked in the office, and they met at work. I remember riding in the car one day; we were going to my grandparents' house so I could spend the night with them. I remember my mother saying, "When we come to pick you up, Jim is going to be your father." I was excited by the thought of having a dad.

Jim was a local race car driver, and we'd spend the weekends during the summer at the race tracks. I'd play during the races, running around getting snow cones and cotton candy, and collecting empty cans from underneath the bleachers. Spectators were allowed to bring coolers into the grandstands and in Michigan there was a ten-cent deposit on each can. I'd run under the grandstands and collect as many cans as I could, many of them beer cans. I became very familiar with the smell of beer, and ironically, to me it smelled nasty!

The memories of loud cars racing around the track, the sounds of wrecks, and the smell of the race track are still among my favorites. Jim never had the fastest car, but he was mine. I would root and cheer as loud and as proud as I could for my "Dad."

A Drinking Problem

Jim was also an alcoholic. I remember him drinking often while working on his race car during the week and before we'd head to the track. After a few drinks, his mood would change. He'd become pretty loud and would hurt people, including my mother and me, with his words while drunk. I realized years later that Jim was the person who first introduced me to the concept of "hurt people – hurt people". I became one of those people who hurt, and went around hurting others as a result of my own pain.

My mother always tried to make a stand against him and his drinking. Once, she even took his car keys, so when he ran out of beer, he wouldn't have any more to drink. It wasn't long after that last beer was gone that we heard the car starting up; mother ran out screaming at him. He was a mechanic after all, so he was able to hot wire the car, and he was on his way to the store to get more beer. What I didn't know as a child, but I do now as a recovering alcoholic is that once an alcoholic sets their mind to getting more alcohol, nothing and no one will be able to stop them!

Despite Jim being an alcoholic, he was still a hard worker. He and my mother both worked hard to ensure that there was never a birthday or a Christmas that I went without. As a child growing up, I remember my mom as always working her butt off to make sure we had what we needed. She is certainly a part of the reason I am a hard worker and a very driven person today.

We never lived in the nicest house or had the best of things, but I knew we weren't dirt poor either. We had enough and life was pretty good. I had a mom *and* a dad. He drank a lot, but I didn't understand what an alcoholic was then. During those years, I thought life was pretty good and I enjoyed having, what to me was, a "normal" family.

Jim was pretty quiet around me. He was always there for me, but was never really willing to talk with me. When I'd ask questions or want to help work on the race car, he was always too busy or didn't want to take the time to help me understand things. He continued to drink daily and the memories I have as a young child often revolve around him drinking and my mother getting mad, with lots of screaming and lots of arguments.

It all culminated one Christmas that I was ten years old. I wish I could erase this memory but I can't. We were driving home from my grandparents' house, where my entire family had gotten together. It was a great holiday, but on the way home my mom and "dad" got into a big argument. It was snowing and blistering cold, and we were driving down a country road in our single cab truck with the wind blowing. I was riding in the middle, with my mom on the passenger side and Jim driving.

He stopped the truck. They argued and argued. He tried kicking us out into the winter's cold as my mother argued back, telling him to drive to the house and: "once we get there, Keith and I are leaving." Arriving home, Jim backed the truck up to the front door and we went inside. My mother said "Keith, go get your stuff from your room and put it in the back of the truck." I was crying as I loaded all the gifts Santa had just brought me the night before. As we loaded the truck with our belongings, I remember seeing things flying from the door into the back of the truck: clothes, blankets, pillows.

As my mother and I pulled away, we were both crying, I was crying because she was crying. I was just a little boy and couldn't help my mother. We drove around for hours, till the night turned into early morning and we returned home, Mom decided we were going back, because she figured Jim had passed out from his drunkenness. We got home and I went back into my bed and fell asleep.

Jim kept drinking through the years. I remember him getting checked into inpatient rehabilitation for his alcoholism. He once went away for 28 days, and we'd often go and visit him. Once he was able to get sober, he walked out of the rehab facility into a 12-step program: Alcoholics Anonymous. Jim chose to be sober, sold the race car, and would focus on going to meetings almost daily.

I was now 12 years old and starting to have my own struggles. I was having a hard time adjusting to who I was and what I looked like. My mother insisted that we start going to family counseling, where we could discuss the hurts and pains, and the toll his alcoholism was having on our family. I know now, but didn't realize at the time, that my pain was also a cause of some of the issues that went on in our home.

His attempt at sobriety took well, and he became very active in his AA group. They opened a meeting house, where he spent a lot of time working to make sure it was nice and comfortable for the members and the newcomers.

My mother also become active in the Al-Anon group, which is for spouses of alcoholics, and I became active in the Alateen group. I wasn't excited at all to be there. The main focus was how it felt in our home when our parent abused alcohol, and the aftermath of the destruction.

I was becoming a young curious teenager myself, dealing with several issues in my own little world. The stress of school, the name calling and bullying were weighing on me. Knowing Jim wasn't my real father, and being a victim of child abuse, were becoming too much for me to handle.

Where was my real father? Why didn't he love me and want to be with me? What did I do to deserve this life of being scarred and not having a father? So many questions and so many people wanting to talk about my feelings, while the only thing I wanted to do was escape, to check out, but I hadn't found a way to do that . . . not yet.

Chapter 3
What Did You Call Me?

"Childhood is the one prison from which there's no escape, the one sentence from which there's no appeal. We all serve our time."

~ P.D. James

All through my school years, I was called names, some of which I still remember. However, my mother had built a strength into me at a young age. When I started school, I'd ask, "What if the kids make fun of my scars? What am I supposed to do?" I was scared.

"Don't worry about the kids who say things about your scars," she'd reply. "A mean man hurt you as a little baby and it's not your fault. I know you're scared and I understand that, but you're special and you have to be stronger than all the other kids. If a kid makes fun of your scars, you have the right to fight back, and you won't be in any trouble with me." That message has stayed with me all my life.

I wasn't called names every day, but when those days came, more times than not, I'd sit at my desk and cry. This was in the younger grades when it was ok to cry. As I got older, the tears turned to fists, and I would get into fights with the kids who called me names. Sometimes, I'd ignore them, close my eyes, and hold it all inside. I'd sit in my desk and block out the entire class. If the teacher was talking, I wouldn't hear a word she said. I would create images in my head of my abuser, not knowing exactly what he looked like. To me he was a monster, and I would think of all the bad things I would do to him. Later I would learn that he was truly a monster!

Recess was my favorite part of school. I was able to separate myself from the kids who called me names and be around the kids who didn't. I spent the first six years of school trying anything and everything in my power to become "normal" in the eyes of my classmates. I thought "normal" was getting girls to like me, being a class clown or class cut-up. By the end of sixth grade, I felt I'd finally accomplished some of that. The names I was called were few and far between, and I felt I had more friends than enemies.

The Scene Changes

The start of Junior High brought with it entirely different and more difficult challenges. Not only were there three elementary schools combined, but there was also a whole class of eighth graders who didn't know me or my story. Of course, I didn't want to tell anyone what had happened to me as a baby. I didn't want people to feel bad for me. I wanted them to like me, whether I looked different or not.

At this age, the social dimension drives the majority of all decisions, as a boy goes from finding girls yucky to finding them a little more interesting, and where you fit on the social ladder impacts every aspect of the day. While I'd often hear other kids call me names, it was no longer "okay" for me to cry, as adolescents were transitioning from boys into young men. It was also a time when the fights that kept breaking out when we were kids began happening less often as we were growing up.

I wanted to fit in with my classmates; I wanted to be funny, I wanted to have girlfriends, and I wanted that "normal" feeling, where I was just one of the kids. I felt if I could win some friends I'd be able to be "normal." My mother had always put a focus on me being as social as I could be. I was always enrolled in baseball, basketball, and bowling. I was never the best at sports but it allowed me to be around more kids. The more kids I was around, the more "normal" I became.

Enjoying The Pain

At the age of 13, I had my first taste of alcohol. That's not as surprising as it may sound at first. In fact, according to a study by the National Institute on Drug Abuse reveals that young boys and girls first taste alcohol at the average age of 12! Once again, I wasn't unique, I was pretty spot on with the statistics.

It was a taste I'd crave for the rest of my life. It was before a dance at my junior high school. One of my friends had his older sister buy a pint of whiskey. We both had that initial taste. I took the first drink, and then my friend did, but he immediately spit his out and wondered how I could drink that stuff. I enjoyed the pain, the burn of the whiskey. We each took a couple of more pulls from the bottle and threw the rest into the yard next to the school.

I went into the dance on Cloud Nine. It was my first time drunk and I didn't get sick. It made me feel neutral, almost numb, and, for the first time in my life, my guard was down. I was no longer Keith Edmonds, the kid who looked different, the kid who held onto so much confusion and anger. I was free of all the burdens placed on me so many years ago by my abuser. For the first time, I felt I didn't have to be Keith Edmonds, the child abuse survivor. I could finally take off the "cape" I so proudly wore to prove to others that I was strong enough to handle what life had thrown at me. And not having to wear that "cape" gave me a new sense of freedom, a sense of strength and a new feeling of confidence.

After that dance and that night, my main concern was how I could continue to feel that way. How could I get more of the alcohol that allowed the feelings that weighed so heavily on me to disappear? Every time I faced conflict in my younger years, I'd continue to find a way to get my hands on some alcohol.

The conflict could be as simple as getting yelled at by a teacher in school, coming home and seeing my mom and stepdad fighting, or some kid at school making fun of me for looking different. Each and every time the alcohol touched my lips, I was able to check out. I didn't have to deal with my emotions and my inner thoughts of anger and pain. My mother was another challenge; she was tough as nails. She's always seen things in black or white; to her, there is NO grey. When I say "no grey", I mean none, ever! To this day my mom doesn't see grey, not *one* shade! How could I do this balancing act between drinking and not having her find out? I knew if I got caught she'd unleash *Brenda hell* on me!

Trouble Ahead

These were tough years for me. I started to feel more anger toward my abuser, and the questions that kept surfacing were getting louder and more intense. "Why me?" "What did I do?" and "I don't deserve this life sentence of looking different that he gave me." The louder the questions became, the more I'd act out, I didn't care about academics at that point; what mattered to me was being cool. My attitude dictated what I did, when I did it, and how I did it.

I had a couple of guys I hung out with – Terry and Tim. We were more on the trouble side than the good side of the school. We had most of our classes together, and spent most of the time laughing and causing trouble.

I remember one time when we were spending the night over at Terry's house. His parents were never really home much and that gave us free rein to get into all kinds of trouble. Whether it was walking the streets through the night or drinking, there was no accountability. One spring night, we walked over to a local drugstore and decided we were going to steal gum, baseball cards, and alcohol.

We walked in with our baggy jackets on and went in separate directions. As I walked the aisles, I'd look around the corners and behind me. I saw

Terry loading his jacket with baseball cards. I grabbed a bottle of whiskey and slid it into my pants. As I walked to the door, I passed Tim, who was loading up with gum. Once outside the store, I took off running until I couldn't run anymore. Tim and Terry caught up with me; we had baseball cards, gum, and booze. We spent the rest of the night in Terry's room, drinking the whiskey, laughing and telling stories.

I'd start stealing stuff even when I was by myself. Any time I was in a store, I'd take a look at something I wanted and would make it mine. As the months went by, I went from stealing booze to stealing clothes.

While at school, my reputation of being cool kept growing, but my academic life remained in the gutter. The heat I was getting from the teachers, and also the principal, continued to intensify. Whenever I did anything wrong in class, the teacher would tell the principal, and he would call my mother. He called my mom *every single time* I did something wrong throughout my Junior High years; and in all honesty:

it was daily! I am certain my mom was on speed dial on the principal's phone and she did not look forward to his calls!

I was clearly acting out, and all I wanted was someone to take the time to understand what I was going through. The principal didn't help; the more he called my mother, the more I'd act out.

Tim, Terry and I continued our thieving ways, until one Sunday when it came to an end. We were hanging out at Terry's, got bored, and decided we'd go back to the drugstore and steal some more stuff. Once in the store, we split up, and began grabbing what we could. As Tim and I finished and headed for the door, Terry was somewhere behind us. Suddenly, we heard a man yell "Hey, STOP! I know you guys are stealing!" Tim and I took a look at each other, ran in separate directions and met back in the field between the drugstore and Terry's house.

As we waited for Terry, the minutes went by, which felt like days, and the more the time passed, the more we started to believe he'd been caught. We also realized we were locked out of Terry's house; he had the key. We had to go back and look for him. We unloaded all the items we'd stolen and headed back toward the store. As we got closer, the man we'd heard yelling at us earlier suddenly appeared, grabbed us, dragging us into the store and into a backroom; there sat Terry.

We were left alone until the store manager walked in with a police officer, who made sure we had no weapons or stolen items. The manager asked for our parents' phone numbers. I knew my parents weren't home, but he told Tim and Terry's parents that no charges would be filed against us. Tim's parents agreed to pick me up and take me home. When I got there, I was alone with my thoughts for hours and hours, knowing I was in serious trouble. I just wished mom and Jim would get home so we could get on with the punishment I was certain I'd receive.

Finally, as day turned into night, I saw head-lights pull into the driveway. I took a deep breath as I heard the front door open.

Crime And Punishment

As they walked in, I sat there on the couch staring at the TV. They greeted me and acted as if nothing had happened. Was it possible I could avoid getting into this much trouble without any consequences?

Once they settled in for the night, my stepdad went out to the garage, where he spent most of his time. My mother sat down and asked how my day was and what I did with my friends. I knew I couldn't hide my guilt. I told her my friends and I got into trouble, and got caught stealing.

I've never forgotten the look on her face and the anger I heard in her voice after I confessed. She told me she already knew and was waiting for me to admit it. Then she went into the disappointment she had in me. She was my biggest fan, and now she was in tears.

"I taught you better than this, Keith Duane. The path you're on right now, your struggles at school with the teachers and even the principal, and now you're showing no respect for any kind of authority. This path is going to lead you to juvenile detention."

That was my biggest fear. I was afraid those kids would show no mercy on me in making fun of the scars on my face. It was hard enough at school but to be placed in with other kids who didn't give a damn terrified me. She kept yelling, and the more she yelled, the more anger and disappointment I heard in her voice. She kept asking me what was driving this behavior, but I never wanted to talk about my feelings. I was always tough enough to handle any situation that was thrown at me. I wasn't about to break now and tell her I couldn't handle all the pain my abuser caused me all those years ago.

I felt part of it was her fault, but I sat there quietly and listened. She told me that when I was a baby, she had to go through the court system to get custody of me, and had to go to parenting classes when I was in foster care, and didn't want to lose me, after fighting for me. She told me she loved me and wanted nothing but the best for me.

"Keith," she said, "you really are your own worst enemy. You're smart, I know you are, even though your grades don't show it. There are plenty of people who love you, and you're strong, one of the strongest people I know. You can get through this; I'll be by your side the whole time."

As the conversation was coming to an end, I thought the lecture was over and I could get back to my ways the next morning. How wrong I was! Mom immediately began spelling out what I would learn as "Brenda's Law." As I sat there, she spelled out my punishment right in front of me.

"First: none of your friends will be staying the night here, nor will you be staying the night anywhere else for the next six months."

"Mom, that's not fair," I yelled, but she was just getting started.

"Second: go into you room and bring out your TV and your stereo."

"Mom, come on! Please don't do this!"

"Third: you're grounded for the next two months."

"Mom, can I at least play with my friends from the neighborhood?" Her one word reply: "Nope."

"Fourth: you've lost all of your phone privileges." In the early 1990s, as a teenager, your phone was your lifeline to popularity; it made you so cool.

At that point, the anger grew inside of me and I checked out. There was no fight left in me as I sat there and listened to her take more of my privileges away. There was still more of "Brenda's Law" to come.

"Each night," my mother said firmly, "you'll sit at the kitchen table and write out the Ten Commandments from the Bible, one hundred times a night for the next month."

"I have to write the Ten Commandments from the Bible?" I would ask, in almost a confused state of mind. Where did she come up with this one? I can understand the others, but this one was far off base. I said "Okay, but why?" As a family, we never discussed the presence of God in our daily lives and we surely never opened a Bible.

My mother, even though not a regular church-goer, does believe in God. She said: "Keith, you not only stole from a store, but you broke one of the Ten Commandments from God: 'Thou shalt not steal.'"

Just like that, the punishment for the crime was laid upon me. As I got up from the couch to go and get my electronics from my bedroom, she said:

"Keith Duane, I'm your biggest fan, I always have been and I always will be. But you have to understand that there are consequences for your actions. This is an important lesson you need to learn, because one day you're going to grow up to be a man and at that point I won't be the one punishing you. It will be your boss or a judge and there's nothing I can do then. You have plenty of people who love you and support you, and it's time you realize it."

As I went to bed that night, I lay there in the darkness and thought about the punishment my friends probably received. I figured they'd get the hammer thrown at them just the way I did. At school that next morning I asked them about it. Tim was grounded for a week and Terry was grounded just for that night. As I walked to my first class, I remember feeling that I got the short end of the stick. That's when I learned that not all people are punished the same for the crimes they commit.

As unfair as I thought my punishment was at the time, I'm thankful today for it. It was a lesson of understanding that my actions not only affect me but they affect others as well, and that, at some point, and in some fashion, there will be a price to pay.

Chapter 4
My High School Years

"I think you accidentally learn things in high school that turn out to be life lessons when you are able to step back a bit and study them in more depth."

~ Megan Fox

Getting through high school was a truly challenging task. While dealing with my anger, and trying so hard to fit in, my focus was not on academics; they held no interest for me. I was there for the socializing and the parties, unaware of the surprises that awaited me.

It was the last summer weekend of 1993, just before I'd be starting my sophomore year. I was just weeks away from turning 16 and getting my driver's license. Being able to drive would be my first taste of freedom, and I was excited about it. My mother had taken our motorhome and gone up north with some of her girlfriends from Al-Anon. My good friend Scott and his family had invited me to join them for a getaway weekend, leaving Jim, my stepdad, alone at home with some freedom of his own.

I was about to head over to Scott's house. It was about three miles, and I was planning to ride my bike, as I usually did. Then, surprisingly, my stepdad offered to drive me, because there was a storm moving in. We loaded my things into his car and off we went. At one point, Jim reached into his wallet and gave me a twenty-dollar bill, saying: "Don't tell your mom about it, and enjoy yourself this weekend."

It was really odd that he'd give me money. Normally I only got my allowance and never anything extra, especially from him. He dropped me off at

Scott's and told me he'd see me on Sunday. "Have fun," he said, as he was leaving. Scott and I loaded my stuff into his parents' van and off we went. We got to the campground that night and set up camp. After building a fire, and having supper, his parents settled in, and then we were off walking around the campground looking for other kids, or girls is more like it. We met a couple of girls that night and spent some time walking around with them.

On Saturday morning, we went tubing down a nearby river. When we got back, I went to the campground office to call my stepdad, but the phone just rang and rang. I thought it was odd but didn't pay much attention to it, knowing I'd try again later. When I did, I got the same result. I started to worry a bit and had a feeling that something was a little off. Where could he have gone? Why wasn't he answering the phone?

No Goodbye

The next morning, we started to pack up and get ready to go home. I was excited, and looking forward to telling my mom and stepdad about the great weekend I had with Scott's family. As we got to my house and pulled into the driveway, I noticed that the garage was super clean, and there was my "new" car waiting for me to drive it. It was a 1980 Volkswagen Rabbit-Diesel with a crank moon-roof, but to me it was a shiny new Cadillac, the best of the best. I barely noticed how bare the garage looked.

When I walked through the front door and into the family room, I was surprised to see it was all re-arranged and some things were missing. With every step, I noticed something was wrong. I hollered for my mom and heard a friend of hers say from a distance "We're in here, Keith!" As I turned the corner into the living room, I saw my mom sitting in the re-cliner, crying. It was the only furniture in the room. The tables, chairs, sofa, TV, and photos were all gone.

As I took a look around, I knew what was wrong. No wonder he hadn't answered the phone. He was gone, taking most of the things we had in our home. I said to my mom, "He's gone, isn't he?" All she could do was cry and nod her head. Here I was, about to turn 16, and my mother sat in a recliner crying and hurt. I couldn't find words to console her, and all I could do was hug her.

I walked from room to room, finding more items gone. I didn't understand how someone could up and leave, with no "Goodbye," no "I love you," not even a "See you later." I guess I got my "See you later," when he dropped me off a couple days earlier. I was both angry and hurt at the same time, but had no outlet to let these emotions out.

Jim had essentially been my dad since I was four years old. He never adopted me, but my name was legally changed when I was in the first grade, so I have his last name. I was almost 16 when he walked out of our lives for good. There were no reconciliation for him and my mom. He was just gone. I had a few interactions with him over the years. I saw him a few times and talked to him some, but there was never any closure to his leaving us so abruptly.

In the spring of 2016, I connected with his son, my stepbrother, Jimmy, via Facebook. I had lost track of Jim over the years, but enjoyed catching up with Jimmy. He and I spoke on the phone and I found out that Jim had cancer and the outlook was bad. Jimmy and I had a good conversation and I asked him to give Jim my number.

I wanted to speak to Jim before he died, but I wanted it to be his choice. He called me in September. We didn't talk about his leaving, we just caught up. I was able to tell him all about the Keith Edmonds Foundation which had been founded in April of that year. I wanted him to know that I had started an organization to help children that we like me when I was younger. It was a good conversation. Jim died in December, and there was no funeral. He was of the mind that if you wanted to see him, you should have done so when he was alive, so it was his desire that there not be a funeral. For twelve years of my life, Jim was my dad, and essentially, he was the only dad I ever had.

Wrestling

One thing in high school that got my attention was wrestling. It was a place where I could finally let out some of the built-up anger in me, but it took a while. In my freshman year I managed to win only one match – all season. It was brutal. Being under-weight had definitely put me at a disadvantage. But my sophomore year was different – for many reasons.

Over the summer, I'd grown a little bit and had added some weight, and we'd gotten a new wrestling coach, "Coach B", who was also my biology teacher. When I first met him, he seemed tough as nails, a very no-nonsense type of guy, young and small in stature but as strong as they come. As I'd discover, his strength wasn't just physical; he was also a strong-willed coach and challenged you to comply. He was also strong in his Christian faith, and still is.

Later in the fall, we had our first wrestling team meeting, and Coach B had made it clear that if you were interested in being on the team, you had to be there. He told us we'd start a pre-training regimen before the season began, running and working out. The first time we had this practice, he took me aside and asked me: "Do you need to put anything on your face to help you sweat? WHAT?!?? What kind of question was that? "No, I don't!"

To make matters worse, he then asked me about my scars – this new guy comes in and is asking me direct and blunt questions. Didn't he know I'd spent years trying to push the questions away, trying to blend in with my classmates and teachers, where I was just a normal kid? I ran off and joined my team-mates on our three-mile run, thinking to myself, who is this guy? Who does he think he is, asking me those questions?

I later found out exactly who he is, a loving and caring teacher/coach who'll push you like you've never been pushed before. He'll hold you accountable for your actions, will be stern when it's needed but will also be your biggest fan along the way. That's something that has stuck with me over the years.

As I work with children and young adults every day, most of what I tell them and the way I treat them was instilled in me by that young teacher. I called him "Coach" then and I call him "Coach" today, but most importantly, I call him a friend.

Life After Jim

After Jim left us, mom and I tried to settle into our new life without him. It was a hard transition for both of us. Because of Jim's sudden, unannounced departure, she was riding an emotional roller coaster, while I was riding a coaster of my own. Having just gotten my driver's license and a car, I was enjoying some new found freedom, and I was taking advantage of it! At the same time, my mom was going through the trauma of her divorce. We were on a collision course.

It wasn't long before we collided. At 16 years old, I found myself kicked out of the home I had known since I was just a little kid. Mom had rules. I didn't want to obey her rules. She said I couldn't live in her house if I didn't follow her rules. So I moved in with some neighborhood friends and their parents. I wasn't far from home and could still visit my mom when I wanted. Sometimes I would see her out the window when she passed going home from work. This didn't last long. Within a few months I was back home where I felt I belonged.

At this point I had allowed my grades to deteriorate so badly and I really didn't care much about anything, anyone, or myself. I had to miss going to wrestling camp because I had to go to summer school, because I did hope to someday graduate with my class. I started working at the local grocery store.

Between school, work, and wrestling practice, I didn't have much time for getting into trouble, or so I thought.

Before long, I found myself kicked out of the house once again. Obeying mom's rules just wasn't very easy for me. This time, Coach B and his wife took me in, and I finally had some structure in my life. I had to ride to school with him, have wrestling practice with him, and go to church with him and Michelle on Wednesday nights, Sunday morning, and Sunday night. The structure they provided, along with talking about my future really got me thinking about what I should be focused on instead of what I was focused on.

My mom would pick me up twice a week and we would go out to dinner and go shopping. We actually enjoyed our time together. She always attended my wrestling meets. Eventually she saw how much I had grown and I was invited to come back home to live with her again. From that point forward, we started building a new relationship. I was Keith, and she was Brenda, trying to focus on being both a parent and a friend.

Zero Hour

During this period of time, I was focusing more on my wrestling. It was the thing that got me through high school. Well, that and alcohol. Times were often tough for me and Coach during the next few years. He was my teacher, mentor, coach, friend, and my father figure. It was a lot on him, and I suppose I never thought of it that way. I am thankful that he was in my life during these years. I shudder to think how things might have turned out if Coach B hadn't been there for me.

One day, at the end of wrestling practice during my junior year, he called me into the coaches' room and told me something that was hard to hear. "The way your grades are looking," he said, "you aren't going to graduate." When I was in school, you were eligible to wrestle as long as you didn't have more than three F's on your progress reports or report cards.

I'd been able to get by that rule, and during my junior and senior years, I was the team MVP. The summer between those two years, I was in summer school making up credits, instead of going to the wrestling camp I wanted. Then, as my senior year began, I found out about something called Zero Hour.

At school, our days were broken into seven different hours, a different class each hour. I remember thinking to myself, what's this Zero Hour? Well, you could make up a credit by taking a class one hour before school actually started. Who does that? Well, I found out I do that, along with going to night school, which also allowed me to make up a credit.

After completing the credit recovery mountain of Zero Hour, night school, summer school, and staying on top of my current classes, whether or not I'd qualify to graduate boiled down to one class. Ironically enough, the class I needed in order to graduate was English, which I'd always hated. Honestly, I'd gotten to the point where I didn't care for the teacher either. So I had dug myself a hole, and I didn't know if I could get out of it, or not. As the semester neared its end, I spent more time focusing on getting that D grade in English; for me D equaled diploma.

Ultimately I would get my D, pass senior English, and graduate with my class. But prior to my finding out if I would indeed graduate with the Class of 1996, I had one more big thing I was looking forward to: the Senior Sleepout - a tradition that we were all excited about!

Senior Sleepout was a long-standing tradition at my high school that took place about two weeks prior to graduation. The members of the graduating class would gather for a final celebration of our four years together before starting a new chapter in our lives. It was like a rite of passage into adulthood. You'd hear whispers through the halls about the legend of the Senior Sleepout. What we didn't know was that for the Class of 1996 it would indeed become legendary for all the wrong reasons, and it would also become a tragedy – a tragedy that would change lives forever.

Chapter 5
My Friend "Sig"

"How lucky I am to have something that makes say-ing goodbye so hard"

-Winnie the Pooh

B ack in first grade, I'd made a friend. It began a friendship which would last through the years from childhood to young adult. Eric John Sig-ulinsky, "Sig" was a little guy, much like me, and he was funny and cool in my book. He played the saxo-phone and one day in the fourth grade he played for show and tell. He played the University of Michigan fight song, and I thought that was the coolest thing ever!

However, it was our differences that would bind us together. Sig was adopted and he was Korean; he looked different than everyone else. He wasn't disfigured like I was, but we were outcasts together, always there for each other. We competed over everything. Competition was a foundation of our friendship, and it was always friendly competition. Each year we would sign each other's yearbook with a tag line, something like, "I'm one inch taller than you!"

That competitive spirit was also evident in school sports. Sig starred on our hockey team, while I did the same in wrestling. As our senior year and high school was coming to an end, we, along with our whole class was looking forward to a long standing tradition at our high school: the Senior Sleepout. The Sleepout was a night, usually a few weeks prior to graduation where everybody in the class would camp out and basically drink and party all night, then either not go to school the next day or go in late and extremely hung over. It was a rite of passage in our hometown. Kids would even come to school with

Sharpie marker on their arms that was a tally of how many beers and how many shots they had at the Sleepout. To us, it was the coolest thing and now, it was our turn.

At school on the day of our Sleepout, I said to him: "All right, man. We've been competitive all through our school years. Let's settle it by seeing who can drink the most tonight." Sig agreed and we planned to meet at his house after school. As we were about to head out to the party, we discussed riding together or driving separately. I needed to be in class the next morning (or I wouldn't graduate), but Sig didn't, so we followed each other to the party.

The Sleepout was one of those things that was legendary, at least in talk around school. We were so excited because it was our time and we wanted to be a part of those stories that would live on long after our high school days were ended. Little did we know that we would indeed be a part of school history.

Most of our 300-plus classmates were there, celebrating our years together and our coming independence. The cool thing about that night and one that was a bit of a surprise was that there were no clicks, no grudges, and no drama, it was just a party that we all enjoyed. Sig and I were keeping track of how many drinks we each had. As the night went on, we got separated, so I began looking for him to see if he was still standing, and found him asleep in a tent; I had won! I kept shaking him, claiming my victory. As the party started to die down, I went to my car for a few hours of sleep before I had to go to school.

I woke up around six a.m. and made my way back to the bon fire looking for Sig. It was barely crackling, but creating enough heat to keep those around it warm. I found him, sitting near the fire, drinking from a two liter bottle of Mountain Dew and eating *my* Fritos. I told him to hand over my Fritos, and we talked a bit about how much fun we had the night before and agreed it was one of the best times we had ever had. I also had to rag on him because after all, I had won the drinking contest!

I had to get going because it was really foggy and it was a bit of a drive to get to school. So I told my friend goodbye and I left the Sleepout. As I walked to my car, the fog seemed to get thicker and thicker. So much so, that I had a hard time finding my car that I had left just a bit before.

I drove slowly, because I could barely see more than ten feet ahead. Each curve that I came up on was a surprise because I literally could not see them coming up. I came to the intersection of the road I was on and state road, M-57. There was only a stop sign that stopped the traffic on the county road; the state road traffic didn't stop. As I looked both ways I couldn't really tell if any traffic was coming. I made it safely through that intersection and I wondered about the long line of classmates who would be coming along behind me. I hoped the fog would clear some before they started leaving.

I was listening to the radio, driving toward school, and piecing together what had been the best night of my life. It felt like for the first time since most of us were in grade school that no one was trying to fit in. We had let our guards down for one night and there was a sense of community within our class that had never been there before. As I started to get lost in the thoughts, I was abruptly brought back by almost missing a curve on this long and winding country road. I was most excited by the fact that I proved I could out drink Sig! I had finally won the battle.

Just a few minutes after I was celebrating my drinking victory over Sig, the DJ on the radio interrupted one of my favorite songs with the breaking news that there had been a fatal accident at the intersection of McKinley and M-57. The intersection I had made it through not long before. My heart sank knowing it had to be some of my classmates. I remember saying out loud in my car, "Please God, don't let it be Sig."

As I walked into the doors of my school I saw groups of people crying, talking and comforting each other. Minutes later an announcement rang out through the halls, it was the voice of our principal. I will never forget hearing him say, "There was a fatal crash this morning that has affected our student body, four students were in the car, and three of them were killed in the crash. There will be grief counselors here shortly to help all those that may need it."

I remember, feeling numb, no emotion, and feeling alone. How could this be? Sig did not have to be at school, he knew that he was not going to school that day, not at least until later in the day. Nathan was a teammate on the wrestling team, and Bill was always one of my biggest fans, he would always give me words of encouragement throughout the years.

I immediately went to the pay phone to call my mom, but the only words I could get out were, "He's gone," and then the tears took over. I couldn't breathe, while she kept asking me who was gone. I just kept saying it over and over, "He's gone". Finally, I was able to muster up the words, "Sig is gone; he died in a car crash this morning." With those words out of my mouth, I dropped the phone as I hit the floor in a pool of tears. When I grabbed the phone I heard my mom telling me to come right home, that she would leave work and meet me there.

Before I left school I walked down to Coach's room. I smelled like booze and looked like hell, but I needed comfort from the one person at the school I thought could provide it. I walked in his classroom and all I could do was cry. He grabbed me and we walked out in the hall where he immediately began to pray. He prayed for everyone in the wreck, their families, our classmates, the school, and the community. His faith frustrated me because I didn't understand it. I went to him looking for comfort, and I know now that his prayer was his comfort, although after he prayed it felt like he was being hard on me. I wanted to tell him about the night and how great the party was, but he wanted to tell me that my life was headed down a dangerous path. I didn't understand that he had been down these same roads as a young person and he understood that the pain of losing more friends or even my own death would be in my future if I didn't change.

All I remember feeling as I left school that morning was anger, sadness and being alone. This was the first time I had experienced the death of someone close to me. As I pulled into the driveway and parked, I sat in my car and sobbed. I couldn't get the tears to stop. My mother came out, opened the door, leaned in and hugged me, telling me how much she loved me. I was able to muster up a couple of words, "Why? Why would this happen?" "Keith," she said, "I have no answers, I know you're hurting; I am too."

When we walked into the house the television was on the midday news. They were reporting from the scene of the fatal wreck. I fell to the floor, and as I heard the words the reporter was saying it felt as if each one was a knife being stabbed deeper and

deeper into my chest. We spent the rest of the afternoon talking about death. I had never dealt with the
pain of losing someone I loved. I didn't understand
how I could have been at Sig's house not even 18
hours ago and now I'd never see him again. It also
hit me that if my circumstances had been different, if
I had been passing my classes and hadn't been required to be at school that morning, I would have
probably been in that car with those guys. I would
have probably died that morning with Sig. My
mother had no answers, but she understood, and she
listened to what I was saying and tried to understand
what I was feeling.

After gaining some composure, all I wanted to
do was check out. I felt alone on the inside, so I
wanted to be alone. Against my mother's wishes, I
walked out of the house and told her I'd be back. I
needed this feeling to go away. And I knew how to
numb myself.

Remembering Sig – A Note To The Reader

I realize that I have included a great deal about Sig and our final time together. This is purposeful. He was, at the time of his death, my oldest and best friend. The one who understood what it meant to be an outcast and who kept me from feeling so alone during my school years. I hope that by telling his story, I honor his memory. I will forever be grateful that I had a friend like Sig. I also wanted to share that our Senior Sleepout was the last one ever for our high school. After the tragedy of that event, a group of mother's organized a lock-in at the school for the next graduating class as a way of trying to prevent such tragedies in the future.

Chapter 6
Looking For Answers

"We learn more by looking for the answer to a question and not finding it than we do from learning the answer itself."

-Lloyd Alexander

I always wondered about two men: my biological father and my abuser. My mom kept the information she knew about these two men pretty close to the vest and would shut me down when I asked her about them. From the age of four to 12, I had Jim, so there was a man in my life, yet, I wondered about the other two. The one who helped her create me and the one who scarred me for life.

After I graduated high school it was finally time. I was going to get the name of my abuser from my mom and go find him. I had created this monster in my mind and I was ready to confront the monster, and get the revenge I wanted and thought I needed. After much prodding on my part, mom finally gave me both names.

Armed with those names, I started asking around. As it turned out, a friend's dad knew both of them, or at least had known them in the past. When I found this out I had lots of questions for him. He said he had lost track of them, but would see what he could find out. He remembered that the two men had actually been friends when he knew them. I was shocked to learn this bit of information and it only served to light a new fire in me of anger toward both of them. My friend's name was Roo, and after his dad made some phone calls, he gave me an address for the man who had fathered me. I told Roo to get ready, we were going on a mission! I hoped that if I found one, I would get information to lead me to the other. My abuser was my ultimate target.

I set out full of all the years of pent up anger boiling over inside of me. I was 18 years old and I was going to get some answers. With his address in my pocket, a cigarette in my mouth, and Tupac thumping on the stereo in my car, we headed out on the mission! As we headed out, Roo asked, "Are you sure you're ready for this?" "Oh, I'm ready," I replied. "I just hope he is, I'm ready to make this situation right."

The address led us to a dilapidated trailer park. When we arrived we found a pretty dismal looking place. It was definitely worse than I was expecting. We were looking for trailer #23. This was another of those Michigan winter days. It was bitterly cold and the snow that was falling only made it look bleaker. Each trailer we passed had blankets up as curtains, and old, beat-up car sitting outside. We found #23, and I pulled into the rough patch of grass that pretended to be a driveway.

I walked up the front steps, and banged on the door, loudly and proudly. I was ready to announce myself and ask my questions without fear. There was no answer, so I knocked again, even louder, until I realized my knocks, no matter how loud, would go unanswered. I felt let down once again. I had mustered up my courage and anger to meet my biological father and track down my abuser, and here I found myself standing on the steps of this dump of a trailer, knocking on a door that was never going to be answered.

As we climbed into the car and got ready to leave, two young boys, and a girl who looked about 12, came barreling around the corner of the trailer. She asked, "Are you Keith?" I was shocked. My mind was racing. Who was she? How did she know my name? But all I could manage to say was the name I had been given of my biological father, and to ask if he lived there.

She said, "He used to, but my mom kicked him out." "Do you know where he lives now?" I asked. I had barely said the last word out when the smallest boy said, "I do, I do. He lives at grandma's house."

"Do you know where that is?" I responded just as quickly. "Yes, up there," as he pointed off into the distance. Then the girl gave us detailed directions. When she was done, I asked how she knew my name. She said, "He talks about you all the time."

Within minutes, we were at "Grandma's house." When I knocked on the door, it slowly cracked open and behind it stood a woman about 60 years old. I asked her: "Does Wes live here?" "He does," she replied, "but I haven't seen him for a couple of days." Facing rejection yet again, and feeling the emotion of the moment, I demanded, "When you see him, will you tell him his son came looking for him?" At that moment, her eyes widened as she exclaimed, "Oh, my God, it's you." The tone of her voice and the expression on her face told me very quickly that this was not the happy discovery of a grandmother finding a long lost grandchild. She wasn't the least bit happy to see my scarred face or hear my angry voice.

Despite her displeasure at finding us on her doorstep, she invited Roo and me into her house. We sat on a worn and dirty couch as she told us stories of my father's inability to grow up, his addictions to drugs and alcohol, and his run-ins with the law. He spent much of my lifetime getting in and out of jail, for everything from drunk driving to drug possession. The way that she made it sound, I was really better off with my mother shielding me from him.

I also heard about how much he loved me and wanted to be in my life, even though he knew he couldn't keep it together long enough to make that happen. "Grandma" also told me the two young boys we had met earlier were actually my half-brothers. Not knowing my father, I never knew I had brothers; it blew my mind.

As the stories went on, I continued to push. "Where's Wes now?" I asked. After she sidestepped the question a couple of times, I pressed for the last time. "Well, I'm here to find some answers and, if you don't tell me where he is, I'll keep coming over until I cross paths with him. I need to talk to him." Finally, she told me he'd been released from jail a couple of days earlier and she hadn't been in contact with him since then.

Back in the mid-1990s, one way to communicate with people was through a pager and a pay phone. I left my pager number with her and told her I had voicemail set up, so if I didn't respond, it would prompt him to leave a message. She said she'd give it to him when she saw him again.

Later that evening, when I was paged, I heard: "Keith, Hello, Keith, are you there? This is your dad. Keith Duane, are you there? I guess not. Okay, if you get this, I'm at my mom's." I walked back to the car, and told Roo to hold on, we were going back.

Meeting "Dad"

We walked up to the door and, as it opened, there stood my father. He said "Hi, son." I said, "Um, hi." As I got closer, he gave me a hug. The smell of whiskey was a stench that will live with me forever. He said "Aw, look at you, you have a receding hair-line, just like good old dad." My first thought was: "You don't even know me, you were never around. How could you ever call yourself a dad, let alone my dad? You were never there for me. You've caused me so much pain." But still it felt good to finally see him.

As we sat there, he'd ask me questions that made me believe that, even though he was absent, he still loved and cared for me. He told me how he'd often drive by the house I grew up in, and how he wanted to be a part of my life, but knew my mother would never let that happen, because he could never keep it together long enough.

He told me how he followed my wrestling career through the newspapers and how proud he was that his son was doing such good things. It was hard to follow his stories, and he was obviously wasted, and it was hard for me to decipher what was true and what the alcohol was saying. As he kept talking, my anger grew ever stronger, which over time would grow into resentment. All he kept saying was: "I wish I could've, I would've, I should've," but all I heard was: "I didn't, I couldn't make you a priority in my life."

As we got ready to leave, I asked the question that had started me on this mission. "Do you know the man who scarred me for life?" His response was, "Uh, Uh, Uh, yeah, I know who he is, but I haven't seen him in years." I quickly responded: "YOU HA-VEN'T SEEN HIM IN YEARS? Like how many?" He said it had been five years or so. Realizing that these two men had known each other and that my biological dad had actually seen my abuser since he burned me, put me into a fit of rage. I wanted a dad who would stand up for me. I wanted to learn that he had wanted to harm the man who harmed me. I didn't get any of that. I will never know if he ever confronted my abuser about what he had done to me, and this man was too wasted to give me straight answers.

I realized I was wasting my time with him. I said one last thing to him before I left, "You're going to tell me right here, right now, where he is or where I can find him." He replied: "The last thing I heard about him was that he was back in prison; he abused another kid." That one statement ramped up my anger and desire for revenge even higher, if that was even possible. How could that monster have been allowed out of prison after what he had done to me, and been back out in the public to hurt yet another innocent child?

As I prepared to walk out of my father's life, he hugged me. It was a hug I neither wanted nor needed from this man. Maybe he needed it. All I could muster to say was, "Thanks for your time." As we walked to the car, the last words I heard were, "Bye, Keith

Duane!" Our meeting was obviously very different for the two of us. For me, it was about finding information on my abuser so I could locate him and get the revenge I so desired. For my "dad" it was about meeting his son.

The conversation on the way home included me saying things like, "Screw that guy!" Roo just listened and let me vent. I was more frustrated on the way home than I was on the way there. I left with just as many unanswered questions as I had arrived with. Later I would reflect on what he told me about his following my wrestling in the newspapers over the years, and understand that was his way of being a part of my life. Many years later I would come to understand that it wasn't my mother or his desire that had kept me from knowing him all the years of my life: it was his addiction.

A Chance Encounter

I only saw my father one other time. I was pretty excited that particular day, not because I wanted to see him, but because of where I was going. I was heading out of town with some buddies for a party. I stopped at a gas station on the outskirts of town, and as I drove up to the full service station, I did a double take at who was walking out to pump my gas. I thought, there's no way this could be. As he kept getting closer, I kept saying to myself, "Is that? No, it can't be! Yeah, I think it is." As he got to the driver's side window of my truck he said, "Hi, Keith" I said "Hey, how are you?" We continued the small talk as he filled my tank with gas.

When the tank was full, I paid for the gas, and told him to take care. He told me the same and I drove away. As I did, I found myself wishing there was something I could do to help him, but I was deep in my own hurts, habits and hang-ups, and after all, he was the father and I was the child. That was the second and final time I would see my biological father alive.

Chapter 7
The Next Steps

"If you're climbing the ladder of life, you go rung by rung, one step at a time. Don't look too far up, set your goals high but take one step at a time. Sometimes you don't think you're progressing until you step back and see how high you've really gone."

~ Donny Osmond

High School was behind me, my best friend and classmates had died, and I had finally met my biological father. I was at a point where I couldn't see what would or even should come next in my life. I was struggling with finding some direction.

I was working and bouncing around, trying to figure out this thing called adulthood.

I started dating a girl who would change my life forever. People change our lives in many ways, some for the good and some for the bad. She and her family would change my life for the good. I'm not saying it was the perfect home, but they were filled with love and optimism and, most importantly, supportive of not only each other, but also of me.

As young couples typically do, we spent a ton of time together. She was a year behind me in school, starting her senior year while I was trying to figure out where and what I was going to do. She was a smart student, got very good grades, and focused on where she was going. As her senior year was ending, she began talking about going to college. College? She was going to leave me? Leave us?

She and her family started purchasing things for her college dorm. I wasn't against her going; I just could hardly believe it. I thought we were going to get married and build a life in our hometown. I knew, or at least I thought I knew, that her moving 100 miles away was certain to end our relationship. But when it was her move-in day at Central Michigan University in Mount Pleasant, I was glad to help, even though it meant we'd no longer be seeing and being with each other every day.

On the campus, I saw a world I truly never knew existed. It was beautiful and it had everything I wanted for her, an opportunity for a better future. I said to myself: "I'm going to make this happen. I'm going to go to college here, period!" But how was I going to do it?

That year, I spent a lot of time driving back and forth from CMU. I also enrolled at Mott Community College, back in Flint. I was working full-time hours as a seasonal employee for our local department of public works and taking night classes. By the time that academic year was over, I'd received a grade point average of 3.4 and earned 24 credits.

I had one piece of the puzzle put together. Next, I went to see some of the doctors and counselors who had treated me when I was young and asked each of them to write a letter on my behalf. I put all this information into a folder and sent it off to the CMU admissions office.

This was not your ordinary college admissions application. I had collected a huge amount of letters and recommendations from everyone I could think of, and my folder was thick! I knew my track record had not been so good, and all I could do was hope for the best. The odds were low of me getting accepted to CMU, and the odds of me graduating were lower than low!

On July 13, 1998, several weeks after sending it, I was on break from my job of cutting grass at a local cemetery. Sitting in the break room, sweaty and dirty, I decided to call the admissions office, full of hope that the answer would be a positive one. When the woman who answered took a few minutes to get my file, it felt like forever. Finally, I heard: "Mr. Edmonds, you have been accepted to Central Michigan University. We look forward to seeing you this fall."

I could hardly believe my ears. How did this happen? Is this real? I wanted to shout the good news to the world. I want it to be clear: NO ONE believed I would get into CMU, much less graduate! Not my mom, not Coach B, certainly not the friends I hung out with: nobody, natta, zilch. Zero chance of Keith graduating from college! I have found that for myself, the quickest way to assure I will accomplish something is for someone to tell me that I can't!

A new life awaited me. I sat quietly for a bit. Then, realizing I still had work to do, I simply walked outside, got back to my mower, and went back to cutting grass.

Chapter 8
Off To College And Beyond

"The future was uncertain, absolutely, and there were many hurdles, twists, and turns to come, but as long as I kept moving forward, one foot in front of the other, the voices of fear and shame, the messages from those who wanted me to believe that I wasn't good enough, would be stilled."

~ Chris Gardner

❝One day your perseverance will pay off, Mr. Edmonds." Those words were uttered by my Business Law professor at Central Michigan University – I've never forgotten them. It was my first semester being at a university. I was twenty-one years old.

I turned 21, two weeks into what would be my first year away from home, at a University where I was certain I didn't belong, but I was there. Was I up for the challenge? I was, as long as I had my girlfriend with me. With her by my side, I knew I was ready. She would always keep me on track and away from trouble.

I took a student worker job within the Athletic Department, preparing for upcoming games and other events, setting up whatever chairs, tables and other equipment were needed by participants, officials and fans. It was a great job to have on campus. It was a way for me to get plugged into a group of students and be around professionals, athletic directors, and graduate students who were trying get in the challenging field of intercollegiate athletics. The work was easy.

Classes, on the other hand, were far more difficult than what I'd bargained for. Receiving tests back
that I had studied for and for which I was trying my
best, and get less than passing grades on, was dis-
couraging. It happened in class after class. I was in
over my head. My girlfriend would push me to go to
class, but that didn't seem to be enough. The mind
game I was playing in my head was like this: "Well,
Keith flunked out of CMU, just like I thought he
would." The more I heard those voices, the easier it
was for me to spend the majority of my time, when
not at work or in class, at the bar.

When that first semester came to an end, I was
placed on academic probation. This meant that if I
didn't receive a certain GPA for the spring semester,
I'd be expelled. Looking at a future of going back
home and bouncing around was *not* what I wanted. If
I went back home, I knew I would never get out, but
how could I get through this? First, I loaded my
schedule that semester with classes I knew I could
pass. Then I asked my co-workers for advice on who

were the best teachers and what their classes were like.

That's when I found out about Sports Management classes. What? They offer classes in sports? Sign me up. I always loved sports, played sports, and paid more attention to them than just about anything in my life, up to that point. That semester went fast. I found school work more interesting, work was fun, and my partying started cranking up, as more friends were coming of age to drink legally.

When that semester came to a close, I was able to get off academic probation, meaning I'd be returning in the fall to start my sophomore year. But I didn't even want to leave for the summer; I actually cried on the drive home. I was leaving the life I was starting to build of my own up there.

I spent that summer cutting grass for beer money, and counting the days till I'd be returning to Mt. Pleasant, and moving into an apartment. My girlfriend got an apartment a couple of buildings over in the same complex, so we could be close to each other.

Party Time

The day I moved into that apartment, I was ready to party. Cases of beer and pizza boxes were all over the place, all the time. When the fall semester started, I went back to work in the Athletic Department, where I liked everyone. They were kind and accepting of me. I was never asked at any time what happened to my face. I was able to function as a normal student worker – one would work his butt off for you.

My motto at this time: "Work Harder – Party HARDER." It wasn't long until my partying, and hurting people with my actions and words, would catch up with me. This time the victim of my wrath was my girlfriend. I'd be out at all hours, smoking and drinking, and not spending any time with her. If she wanted to see me, there were two choices: when I was at work, or when I was at the bar.

I was so blinded by the partying, I never really noticed that our relationship was coming to an end. She had checked out and it was only a matter of time until the inevitable happened - the breakup. I took the hit hard when she broke up with me. I had to drive by her building every day on my way in and out of the apartment complex. Not understanding why she felt the way she did, one thing I did understand was how I was feeling – alone and angry. These feeling were too much for me to handle. I knew how to make this pain go away: drink until I couldn't see and couldn't feel. I kept going to class, hurting from the night before, sometimes with no or little sleep. I was hung over, but I was there.

During one class, I had a notoriously tough professor. Legend had it if you passed one of her classes, you accomplished something. Each day, she'd call your name to make sure you were in class. One day, she passed around her attendance log instead of calling the names out loud. As it made its way around the room and landed on my desk, I saw a brief note next to each name. Next to mine: "scars on face."

That was enough to set me off. I was furious! How could she have written that next to my name? And, to top it off, pass it around for everyone in the class to see? I went to her office after hours and told her exactly what I thought of that move. I was full of anger and was not holding back. "You call me out? I'm going to give you a piece of my mind."

I got my point across and she apologized. I can make my scars go away in my head, and even once you get to know me, but it felt like no matter which direction I turned, I'm stared at, called out, or made fun of. For what? Crying in the middle of the night when I was a baby? After that meeting, it was time to drink, and drink hard I did. My girlfriend was gone and I felt I was being attacked.

I was drinking to a point of blackout almost every night. More times than not, I'd wake up in my own vomit or urine. I was a 20-something-year-old bed wetter. Yet, at no time did I think I had a drinking problem. This was just normally partying. Each morning, I'd look out the window to see if my car was there and in one piece.

A Dream Comes True

One morning, when I woke up in the pain that had become normal, I remembered I was due to meet with a school official to learn where I stood academically, and how many more credits I'd need to earn my degree. I stumbled into the woman's office reeking of booze.

I was astonished when she said to me: "You have twenty-one credits to complete the requirements for your Bachelor of Applied Arts degree." As I wiped the sweat from my face, which was more than likely liquor from the shots the night before. I said: "That's less than two semesters?" "Correct," she said.

Somehow, and to this day, I'm not really sure how I got that close to graduation. It felt like I woke up from a three-year bender and was about to realize my dream of graduating. But how? All I know is that if I showed up to class as much as I could, the size of the hangover didn't matter. I had to get my butt in that seat during class. It's true what they say; as long as you go to class you're bound to pick up enough information to pass the class. You may not graduate with honors, but you can graduate.

As I did for class, I always showed up for work. If there was an event going on, I signed up and made sure I was there. After some time, I was given more responsibility and was even given charge of some of the other students. It made me feel like I had a home within the Athletic Department. Many of them were not just a work family, they were family, to me anyway. That was something I'd never really had before.

As my course work was coming to an end and graduation was nearing, I learned there'd be an Assistant of Game Operations position available. This was the job I wanted and, on top of that, they wanted me! After graduation, I accepted the job. Here I was a college graduate and working full time in a Division 1 athletic department! Could life get any better, with the same work hours, and then going to the bars where everyone knew my name?

But the good times wouldn't last. During men's basketball season in my first year, I was in charge of the whole student crew and making sure the games went off without a glitch. After one game, I felt the pain I'd spent years trying to avoid. We were playing Xavier University. Our basketball team was very good that year and so was Xavier's. We came out victorious, and I was proud and fired up. I was helping my students fold and stack chairs when a Xavier fan, angry that his team lost, remarked: "Look at you, all scarred up. You're trash, just like this school."

To this day, I can feel my anger. I remember I had to walk away. I was hurt, a kind of hurt that sticks with you. Here I was living my dream, working for a university. I had overcome so much to get to this point and, because this guy was a disgruntled fan, I paid the price. Yet again, another instance in my life where I am reminded that "hurt people – hurt people." Finally, I collected myself and returned to the arena to finish my job.

That fan would stay in my head for the longest time. Before every game, I'd wonder if someone from the opposing team would say something like that to me. It seemed that every time I'd start getting into a comfortable stride in life, someone would comment on my looks and reawaken those painful memories. I did what I always do; I faced it head on, living in fear as I waited for the next time. And there was always a next time! I'd drown it away with as much booze and numbing as I possibly could. I became a functioning alcoholic. I was able to graduate, drinking all the time, and able to work, drinking all the time.

That following spring, I went out with a bunch of friends to celebrate my best friend's birthday. We went to a local sports bar, having lots of booze and lots of laughs. I was well on my way to putting my feelings behind me and enjoying the night. At closing time, we all walked out to the parking lot, and I got into my car. All my friends kept offering to give me a ride home, but I wasn't having it. Like everything else, I was in control and could handle anything thrown my way.

On the way home, I was pulled over, received my first DUI, and was lodged in the Isabella County Jail. During the booking process, they take your mug shot and finger prints, and write down any tattoos or scars. Once they finish, you sign the paper. I remember looking at that paper, SCARS ALL OVER FACE. I started yelling and kicking and screaming. It was all those years of pain coming out.

As it turns out, the officers in booking don't like you yelling and screaming, especially when you're already under arrest for driving under the influence. I was thrown into a jail cell by myself, where I could yell and scream and cry about the pain. They didn't understand that I didn't deserve this. How could anyone handle the stuff I'd been through? Finally, my screaming and banging started to taper off, and I passed out on the floor.

When my court date came, I was found guilty of DUI, with a blood alcohol level of .23, almost three times the legal limit. I had to attend Alcoholics Anonymous meetings, have a substance abuse evaluation, lost my driver's license for 60 days, had to pay a driver's responsibility fee of $1,000 a year for two years, couldn't be in any establishment that served alcohol (I went anyway), one year of probation, and had to attend Impact Weekend, which I knew nothing about.

I soon learned it was a weekend of counseling and work, when you checked in on a Friday and checked out on Sunday. It was held a couple of hours away, so I scheduled it for when I got my license back. I arrived in mid-August to serve my time at Impact Weekend. Upon arrival, you turned your keys in, realized you were there for the long haul, and you had no chance of leaving until it was over.

We spent the weekend learning of the effects of drinking and driving, heard from families who had lost loved ones to drunk drivers, and were warned about the dangers of doing drugs. Once Sunday afternoon arrived, we were free to go. All I had to do was keep it together and get off probation.

On the day I got back to my house, I received a call from my mother. She kept saying she had something to tell me but didn't know how. Over and over, I'd hear it. Finally, she said, "Your biological father died." She asked if I planned to attend the funeral or at least go to the funeral home. I told her, "Nope, no interest, whatsoever." Since I never really knew my father, my reaction was simple: "It sucks to be him," and for me, that was that.

I have an uncle, my mom's brother, who is only six years older than me. I think of him as a brother. I was talking to him about the whole situation and asked if he thought I should go to the funeral for the father I never knew. He said that if I didn't, I'd likely regret it someday, and suggested I attend the viewing at the least. So I agreed to go to the visitation, as long as he'd go with me.

We went to the funeral home where, for the first time, I met several members of my biological father's family, including my half-brothers and aunts. My "grandmother" made a big deal of introducing me to all these people as "Michael's son". That felt both weird and awkward to me. Many of his close friends said they didn't even know he had another son, until they saw my name listed in his obituary. Looking back on that experience, I understand why my uncle suggested I go and I suppose in some ways I am glad I did, but at the end of it all, Michael was never my dad.

After a night of meeting people from my father's side of the family, I went where I always go when life gets too heavy – the bar. Not even just a couple

of hours removed from Impact Weekend, I was back
at the bar.

Chapter 9
On The Move

*"If you don't know where you're going, any road
will take you there."*

~ Lewis Carroll

In the fall of 2004, I resigned from my position at
Central Michigan University. I'd found myself at
another of those junctures where I knew something
had to change and I left Mount Pleasant. I had no idea
where I was going, but I knew I couldn't stay where
I was.

I drank every day, I got drunk every night, and I
woke up with a hangover every morning. I was just

like so many others who find themselves at a place in life where all they want is to run away from what their life has become, or what they've allowed it to become. I wanted a geographical solution to my internal problem. I thought fixing the outside might fix the inside. Of course I was wrong – again. So I moved back to Flint and bounced around for about six months, looking for jobs, drinking, and generally wasting my life.

Then I found a job – in Omaha, Nebraska. Yep, Omaha! Why there? Besides the fact that I had one friend there, I didn't have an answer to that question. Regardless, I packed up all I owned, put it into a U-Haul trailer, and drove 900 miles to the Great Plains of the USA. I got a job with Omaha's American Hockey League team, but was only there for a few months, and to be very honest, I hated it.

I found an apartment, which happened to be just across the street from a little neighborhood bar. So I started my new life, in a new place, with a new bar just steps away! The job with the hockey team didn't turn out to be a good fit for me, so I quit and took the first job I found. It was perfect for me because I was an expert on the product – it was at a beer company. Life was becoming good again. I was partying pretty hard, but I was able to keep it all going, at least for a while. I started going to the little bar across the street more and more often.

At first I went because it was convenient and I was lonely. Of course, I found a waitress there I was attracted to, and the bartenders became my closest friends. Typically, I'd go to the bar after work, arriving about 4:00 p.m., and sit there, drinking and talking, until 2:00 a.m. or so, when the place closed. Then I only had to stumble across the street to my apartment. I became a regular, and part of the "bar family." Although I'd always wanted to be part of a family, this wasn't the family I needed.

I found myself at one of the lowest points of my life during my time in Omaha. I was taking and losing jobs at a rapid pace. I was also rapidly hurting people. I was lonely, despite my new "family," and I found myself sinking deeper and deeper into depression. I wouldn't answer phone calls from my close friends and felt isolated. The darker my world became, the drunker I would get to try and escape the pain I felt.

Under Arrest

In February 2008, I was arrested for an outstanding warrant on a ticket I hadn't paid. After spending the night in jail, I remember walking along the riverside and thinking I'd be better off if I just jumped off the bridge into the Missouri River, knowing I'd drown, and that all the pain of my world would be gone. I entertained the thought of just being done, with all of it, the arrests, the drinking, the mess I was making of my life. Just be gone and be done. Of course, I didn't jump in the river that day, but I'll never forget the way I felt and how badly I wanted to just escape.

As my court date was approaching, I was trying to decide if my time in Omaha was over. Was it time for me to make another move? When I went to court, it was General Sessions Court, and the courtroom was full of people waiting to get in front of the judge to enter their pleas. My name was called fairly early: "the State of Nebraska vs. Keith Edmonds." I walked in front of the judge, hoping for a quick dismissal. As he started to ask me the usual questions: home address, date of birth, highest level of education, etc., I answered quickly.

That Question Again

Then he asked me the question that always threw me off my game: "What happened to your face?" I was stunned! I'm certain the expression on my face was one of anger and disbelief, as all those years of pain came flooding back into my mind. I wanted to shout at him: "Really, you're asking me that in front of thirty or forty other people in this courtroom? Why would you ask me that? It has no relevance to me not paying a ticket."

The anger I felt in that moment made me want to lash out at him. But what would I gain besides another night spent in a jail cell for contempt of court? Nothing! So, begrudgingly, I told him – while all those other people listened in – about the abuse I'd suffered as a baby that had caused my face to be scarred. My case was ultimately dismissed, once I paid the court fines. It was at that point I realized my time in Omaha was inevitably coming to an end.

A couple of weeks later, I sold everything I owned and what didn't sell made its way to Goodwill. I even had to sell my truck. I needed money to pay my court costs and buy a plane ticket. I knew I needed yet another change of scenery to get my life back together. This time, I was moving back to Michigan with no car, no money, and one suitcase full of whatever I could fit into it. I had nothing.

Once I got back to Flint, I started applying for jobs, in hopes of finally getting my life together. After years and years of partying and not caring about responsibilities and obligations, my credit was in the trash and I couldn't get approved for an apartment. So, I lived in an extended stay hotel, which is about as close as you can get to being homeless without actually living on the streets.

Much to my surprise, I landed a pretty good job with the Coca-Cola Company in Detroit. I was an account manager and soon started to make decent money. I was even given a company car. In general, things were looking up, although I continued to drink heavily, and went to work daily with a hangover. I could have been the poster child for functioning alcoholics! But my ways were soon going to catch up with me.

A Close Call

On Friday, May 15, 2010, my buddies and I started drinking about one o'clock in the afternoon. I had taken the day off from work, and we were having a great time starting our three day weekend. Later that evening, I impulsively decided to drive about two hours south to see a girl I knew. One of my buddies and I jumped into my company car and headed south.

About an hour into the trip I blacked out, lost control of the car, and it flipped five times. Sig had died on May 16, 1996, and our Senior Sleepout had been on May 15, 1996. Maybe I was celebrating Sig with my behavior fourteen years later, maybe I was just getting wasted. Either way, I almost shared a death date with my old friend.

I woke up in the Neuro-Intensive Care Unit of a hospital and was told I had fractured my C2 vertebrae. I was still basically wasted when the doctor told me about my injury, and I know now that I wasn't aware of its magnitude. In fact, after learning to my amazement that my buddy had not only survived but was uninjured, I actually tried to laugh it off. The doctor told me he had examined my x-rays closely and I had a hairline fracture. He didn't feel surgery was needed, but that I'd require a long recovery, wearing a Miami-J neck brace. He assured me that in time, I should be fine.

I've since learned that the C2 vertebrae is also called the "Hangman's Vertebrae," which means it's what snaps when a person is hanged. I also learned it's the same injury Christopher Reeve, the late movie actor of *Superman* fame," had suffered when thrown from a horse, although he shattered both his C1 and C2 vertebrae and did significant injury to his spinal cord, leaving him a quadriplegic. I understand I'm not invincible, and by all rights, I should have died in that car accident. Looking back now, there's no doubt in my mind that my life was spared for a reason that night in that car accident.

When I was released from the hospital, I found myself once again trying to figure out what to do with my life. I knew I had to recuperate, but in all honesty, I had expected the police to be waiting to arrest me when I got out of the hospital, but they weren't there. I still had my license, there were no charges pending that I was aware of, and I knew I had seven weeks to figure out what to do next.

For those seven weeks, I lay on a couch. I drank and took my pain pills. I was basically stoned this entire time. Pills were never my drug of choice. I'd take them if I was with a group of people doing them, but my buddies and I were drinkers. The pills helped me get through this recuperation period. As soon as I got to where I could take the neck brace off, I did what drunks do: I went to a bar! Even if I could only have it off an hour or so a day, I would make plans to go to a bar.

Coca-Cola fired me, which was no surprise. So here I was at a crossroads again.

Chapter 10
Home At Last

*"Like a wavering compass needle that points at last
to north, that weather-vane soul of mine had found
the direction it would point to from now on."*

~ *Peter G. Jenkins*

While recuperating from my accident, I still
didn't have a clue what to do next. Then
one day, I received a call from an old college friend
named David. We hadn't talked in some time and he
didn't know about my wreck and injury. I shared
with him about my life, the accident, and where I was
at the moment in trying to decide what to do once I

healed. He caught me up on his life and told me he was going through a difficult time himself.

He was living in Florida, had just lost his job, and was at a crossroads in life. Both a singer and a songwriter, it had always been his dream to make it in the music business. We had talked over the years about moving to Nashville. We had said that we would make that move together. He'd been thinking it was time for him to make the leap and move to the Music City. There was my answer about what to do next. I was moving to Nashville, Tennessee!

Making this move had always been something I had thought about, but hadn't had a reason to make it happen. When I was a kid and going yearly to Cincinnati to the burn hospital, we'd usually take a little side trip on the way home. We'd go to Tennessee. Sometimes it would be to the mountains of eastern Tennessee, sometimes to Nashville.

I have a memory of staying at the Shoney's Inn in Lebanon. Today the building's still there, but the name of the motel has changed. It could just be irony that Lebanon, Tennessee, is the place I now call home, but, I think it's probably more than that. I think the groundwork was being laid, when I was still just a burned kid, for the life that lay in store for me today, living in recovery, and working with the abused and troubled kids of Wilson County.

As I lay on a friend's couch, recuperating and thinking about this move to Nashville, I realized I had just about nothing. I couldn't afford a plane ticket, so my mom bought it, and I packed what little I had into one little suitcase, phoned David to let him know I was on my way, and flew off to Nashville.

I arrived and took an airport shuttle to a nearby motel, and spent my first night in the state that would become the place where I'd finally rebuild my life. Meanwhile, David had been driving through the night from Florida. He picked me up and we went and found an apartment. It wasn't much because we neither one had much, but we were in Nashville, Tennessee, and we were starting a brand new life!

It was late July, 2010, and there we were in what some folks called "NashVegas." What more could an alcoholic ask for? With bars (they call them "honky-tonks" in Nashville) on every corner, and all in between, once again my plan to rebuild my life would have to wait. Little did I know the rebuilding was still a few years in the future, but that I had arrived in the place where that building would happen.

We immediately started hitting the bars, and we had plenty of time to hit them all. My partying ways were continuing as if nothing had happened back in Michigan. I was getting blackout drunk, waking up in my own filth, going from woman to woman while hiding my true self from them, getting jobs, quitting jobs, losing jobs, and always being hung-over. From the summer of 2010 until the fall of 2012, that was my life. Same old crap, different location, and with more bars!

A Double Birthday

Earlier in this book, I talked about the day I stopped drinking. It was my 35th birthday, September 9, 2012. I celebrate the day I was born and the day I entered sobriety, on the same day each year. It's a double birthday! On that day in 2012, I was sitting in my car alone, drinking my third, 22-ounce Coors Light Beer, listening to music. I had hurt someone the night before, and I was wallowing in the guilt and shame of it.

I was tired of it all. I was contemplating my life, where it was, where it had been, and where I wanted it to be. This was my rock bottom. I said out loud in that car, "God, I don't even know if you are there, but if you are, I need help." I opened the car door and poured what was left of that beer out on the pavement. By God's grace, that would be my last drink.

The next day I found the location of an Alcoholics Anonymous (AA) meeting. I was sitting in the parking lot and I didn't want to go in. I didn't want to be like "those people." Did I really belong there? I mean, I liked to drink and party but, in my eyes, so many people had worse problems than I did. I figured, for the first time in my life, I'd voluntarily go to a meeting and prove to myself I didn't belong there.

As I sat there in my car, I watched a few people entering the building. As I tried to dig up the courage to do the same, I found myself judging them as they walked past me. Nope, I'm not as bad as this guy; I could tell by his look. He looked rough. I'm not sure what I thought I looked like, but I knew in my head I didn't look "that bad." As an addict/alcoholic, you never think you're as bad as this guy or that other guy. You continually justify and lie to yourself. That's part of the addiction.

Finally I walked in, but didn't say a word to anyone. People would say hello, but I kept walking until I found the meeting room. Once there, I went to the very back, knowing that if I sat there, I could just listen and leave. When the meeting got underway, the guy right in front of me started talking. He was probably 10-15 years older than I was, and he told his story of wreckage: DUIs, car crashes, hurting people who were close to him, and the pain he'd harbored for so long.

The longer he talked, the more I thought to myself, "Damn, this guy I was judging from my car in the parking lot, his story – while different – is my story." At the end of the meeting, I walked back to my car without saying anything to anyone. I sat there for a while and thought to myself: "Damn it, I am an alcoholic/addict and this is where I belong."

When I got home that night, I was lying in bed, and I kept thinking to myself: "How can I get rid of a lifestyle that has always allowed me to check out and not have to deal with these feelings of being alone, alienated, and angry?"

The next day, I found another meeting to attend. The more meetings I attended, the more I sat there and listened to both younger and older people share their story, it became more and more clear to me that I did, in fact, have a problem and I was right where I belonged.

I reached out to a sober friend, told him what was going on with me, and that I wanted to live without drinking. I asked him to be my sponsor and my partner on this journey I was finally ready to take. I started attending recovery meetings every night, focusing on understanding that I truly was (and am) an alcoholic. My friend recommended that I try a Christ-centered recovery group called Celebrate Recovery. CR is much like the other 12-step recovery programs, except it's completely Christ-centered and includes Scripture that corresponds to the steps.

A few weeks later, I attended my first Celebrate Recovery meeting. This meeting, this group of men, would change my life forever. Every Wednesday for the next five years, you could find me at this meeting. I can actually count on one hand how many times I missed that meeting in those five years. I was usually one of the last people to leave after the meeting ended.

The Coffee Cart

Going to meetings daily became my new routine. I went as if my life depended on it, because I soon realized that it did! I didn't share at first. I just went and listened, and tried to apply what I heard. Then I started to open up a little, and I took on the job of taking care of the coffee cart. Coffee is a big part of recovery meetings! I suppose caffeine becomes the drug of choice for those in recovery!

The coffee cart may seem minuscule to some, but for me at the beginning of my journey into recovery, it was huge. It gave me a purpose and responsibility. I'd get there early and I was the last to leave. I became someone the others counted on, even if just to have the coffee ready. It was accountability for me. I finally had a family I could count on and be accountable to. My life was different and I was actually beginning to enjoy living for the first time.

Once I started going regularly to 12-step meetings, I found that the first step is the one that sticks with me every day: "We admitted we were powerless over our addictions and compulsive behaviors, that our lives have become unmanageable." I had been powerless over my addictions for a long time and my life had certainly become unmanageable by me. Real change happened when I recognized and acknowledged both these things to be absolutely true in my life, and allowed God's power to manage the unmanageable. There is great peace in taking that first step.

Perhaps my favorite quote and one I use often is from the late author, Edwin Louis Cole. He said, "You don't drown by falling in the water; you drown by staying there." I stayed in the water a long time. There were several times when I should have drowned. Even when things were at their worst and I thought I was at the end of my rope, I knew my life was a result of my poor choices. I hated to hear, "make good choices." That's so easy to say, but so hard to do. Choices have consequences. And consequences can be either good or bad.

My sober life today is one of contentment. It took me a long time to understand the difference between being content and being complacent. I lived in complacency a long time. Content means a state of peaceful happiness. Complacent is being pleased with oneself without awareness of some potential danger or deficits. Today I have real friendships and relationships. I am honest, and I correct my mistakes as soon I realize them. I have stability, not wealth, but enough. I do work that gives me satisfaction. I am given an opportunity, almost daily, to have a positive impact on the lives of others, often, young people. I have a sense of belonging and I live in peace in the present.

I still go to Celebrate Recovery. I look forward to going and I don't let other things interfere. I still need to admit to others and myself that I'm broken and in need of help. I spent so many years making geographical changes, but not changing myself. I sought peace that was never going to be found in any bar or in any bottle. Because of CR, working the steps, the people who are part of my sober life, and my relationship with the Lord, I haven't had a drop of alcohol in over seven years!

I also recognize that I can't let my guard down. There's an alcoholic who lives inside of me. I'm still, and will always be, an alcoholic. God's grace is why I'm alive and sober. I have to remind myself of that every day and make a conscious choice, every day, to live in His grace and to continue working the steps of recovery to maintain my sobriety. I can never take that for granted. There are lots of saying in recovery meetings. One of those is, "Just for Today." I wake up every morning and acknowledge that I am an alcoholic and ask God to keep me sober, just for that day. Sobriety does not take a day off!!

Chapter 11
Sharing My Story

"Owning our story and loving ourselves through that process is the bravest thing that we'll ever do."

Brene' Brown

After years of being both the teenager and the man who wouldn't listen to anyone and any good advice, I knew exactly who to call when I got to the point of surrender. I called Coach B. It had been some time since our last contact and it took me a few minutes to find his phone number and make the call. The phone rang, and while I waited for an answer, I wondered how he'd react to hearing from me.

When he answered, his voice was exactly how I remembered it. As soon as he heard my voice, he said, "Keith, how are you, what are you doing these days?" It was like we had never left off.

I told him I was living in Nashville, and that I had recently stopped drinking. I told him I was attending Celebrate Recovery. Coach B was and is a strong Christian man. I told him about the wreckage I had created in my life since we had last talked. I didn't try to clean it up or make it pretty. I was honest and told him of the arrests and the damage I had done to myself and to others. I told him I was planning to live sober. As was always the case, he was one of my biggest fans and supporters. He was excited for me and for my sobriety.

That was Coach. He told me he'd check in on me frequently, and he did just that. We've continued our relationship to this day. I also told him of my plans to share the story of my transition from a child abuse victim to a child abuse survivor.

He said there's power in my testimony and that it could help a lot of other people. He was a big supporter of my early days of sobriety and is a big supporter today. When the Keith Edmonds Foundation held its first Camp Confidence, he came down and helped with the kickoff. It was such an honor to have this man who I so respect, come and be a part of something positive and good that was happening in my life.

When I look back to when I first began to talk about myself and share my story publicly, I'm reminded of how I felt during that time – both crazy and fearful! It seemed crazy that I was going to actually talk, in public, in front of people I sometimes knew, and often people who were strangers, and tell them about my abuse and everything that had happened since then. I always thought of myself as a back-row guy, never a front-row guy! And certainly, not a stand-up-in-front of people guy!

I also remember this undeniable sense of not believing I'm actually going to do this, but also the sense of being ready. It was only through sobriety that I gained the clarity to be comfortable sharing the pain I had hidden and pushed down for so long. It was almost screaming to come out of me. It felt like I was saying to my abuser, "I'm going to take what you did to me and use it. I'm going to take it and flip it!"

But before I could do any of that, I had to go back home to Flint, Michigan, and get the court records, so I could actually see what had been done to me at the hands of my abuser. I had always *heard* what had been done to me, but I wanted the truth of it, and that could only come through the court records. So, I got up one day in Nashville, and drove to the courthouse in Flint. I got there and asked for the court records; eventually, I got them.

Getting my hands on the records, and reading the truth as it came out in court, led me to sharing my story for a couple of reasons. First, because of the anger my abuse had created in me, and second, because I really wanted to help other people by sharing my personal story. There's a well-known comment by Martin Luther King Jr. that resonates with me. He said, "There comes a time when silence becomes betrayal." I could no longer be silent and I didn't want to betray all the other people who were hurting, just as I had for so many years. There are literally millions of us, who are either scarred on the inside or scarred on the outside. I'm one of the lucky few who is scarred both inside and out. I wanted to give others the hope I had found to live beyond my scars.

I spent my whole life *not* telling people what had happened to me. I could tell that people would want to know, but socially accepted politeness would keep most from actually asking. I wanted to tell them, but at the same time, I didn't want anyone to pity me. So, for the majority of my life, I lived without ever telling anyone what happened to my face. There were very few people who ever got close enough to me that I was willing to tell them about the abuse that caused my scars.

It was easy to let others wonder if I'd been burned in an accident, maybe a house fire, or something, anything that could have been just a horrible accident. It seemed better to let them think what they might, rather than share that I was a victim of abuse. So I continually asked myself if I really had it in me to say, out loud, in front of people, that I'm a survivor of child abuse. Today, in my recovery meetings when I introduce myself, I say, "Hi, I'm Keith, and I'm an alcoholic and a survivor of child abuse." And it's only by the grace of God that I can say that naturally, and no longer have a desire to hide who and what I am.

I have felt for a long time that 14 month old Keith lives inside of me, and it is his story that I tell. His life was spared for a purpose. I don't remember him. I don't remember my face without these scars. But he is definitely a part of me and he is the part that gives me the fire and tireless energy that I use to do the work I do today. I've heard that our growth stops at the point we are abused, which makes sense when

I consider people I know who were abused during their adolescents or teen years. I don't know if that is actually true for someone who was abused at a much younger age. Regardless, I will continue to tell 14 month old Keith's story, and use his tenacity.

Armed with the court records, and having a firm sense of the truth of what had happened to me at the hand of my abuser, I was ready to share my story. The very first time I did this was back in my hometown in Michigan. There were posters in the grocery store where I had worked as a kid, and fliers around the town, announcing that I was coming back to Flushing to share my story. I was even interviewed on the local news channel. It was December, and it was an especially frigid winter, and I don't like being cold! It has occurred to me that many of the most poignant events of my life have occurred during an especially cold winter, most of them in Michigan!

The "event" was being held in a little cafe in the downtown area. It was advertised as an opportunity to give back to two community organizations, and to help two families in the area that were struggling. A love offering was taken up for those reasons. Among the thirty-some odd people who showed up were Coach B, several of my classmates' parents, former teachers, Sig's mom, and my mom. That night as I shared my story, I told them that someday I would write a book to share my story with what I hoped would be a much larger audience.

Today I'm more polished when I speak in front of crowds, but looking back I realize that first time I basically aired all my dirty laundry! I also told them of my plans to help others, hopefully countless others, through the sharing of my story. After that, I drove back to Nashville, and the next day, I went back to work, hoping for the next opportunity to share. It was December 2012, and it was my ninety-days-sober birthday.

As I waited for the next opportunity, I did the things I needed to do to maintain my sobriety. I worked the 12-Steps, went to countless meetings, continued my path to learning how to live as a sober person, and created a Facebook page to offer help to other child abuse survivors. Then the big one came. I was invited to attend the Mid-Atlantic Conference for Child Abuse and Neglect, in Annapolis, Maryland, and was asked to be the Keynote speaker.

There I was, on an airplane, flying to another state, to share what was meant for evil that was now becoming good. I could hardly believe this was actually happening to me! The night before I was to speak, I was in my hotel room, which was connected to the conference center, and I was very literally freaking out! So I did what I do when I need encouragement: I called Coach. And he said what he always says, "Hi Keith, what are you doing?" To which I replied, "I'm in this hotel room in Annapolis, Maryland, at this conference, and tomorrow I'm the Keynote speaker and I'm freaking out!" His response was so classic Coach. He said, "What an amazing opportunity you have. Doors are being opened for you."

After talking with him, I felt a bit calmer, but still not really calm. I didn't sleep much that night.

The next morning I woke up, sat in my room, got ready, took a deep breath, walked out the door and down the stairs to the conference, and was introduced. I was handed the microphone and 500 people sat, looking at me. My mind went to an uncomfortable place, and for just a minute, I truly wanted to check-out like I used to do when I found myself in an uncomfortable place. But my days of checking out were done.

It was one of those moments in life where you either have to sink or swim. I swam. I had a PowerPoint presentation I had created to accompany my talk, and I stood before that large audience and told them of the horrific things that had been done to me at the hands of my abuser. I also shared the challenges of adolescence and the destruction I had created in my life as an adult. Lastly, I told them of the triumph of the transition of going from being a victim to becoming a survivor of the terrible things done to me as a child.

When I finished, they gave me a standing ovation. After the session, there was a meet and greet, where a line formed of people wanting to meet me and talk to me. The line went as far back as I could see, and I was overwhelmed by the reception and acceptance I received from these people. This event gave me a sense of conviction that I was doing exactly what I was supposed to be doing, but I still didn't have a clear sense of knowing how I was supposed to do that or what to do next. Sometimes I still don't, but today I just keep doing the next thing, the next right thing, and I do it one day at a time, as I have learned to do in my recovery journey.

Chapter 12
Someone To Bank On

"None of us has gotten where we are solely by pulling ourselves up by our own bootstraps. We got here because somebody bent down and helped us."

~ Supreme Court Justice Thurgood Marshall

After my first big speaking gig, I returned to Nashville and went back to work. One day, I'd been on stage in front of 500 people, and the next day I was back being a sales manager at the merchandising company where I was working. I realized it was time for me to start putting this story down on paper. Over the next several months, I wrote a lot, including much of what you're reading now in this book.

I was also continuing to share my story, anywhere and everywhere there were people interested in having me speak. I spoke at a small Christian university in Missouri, at the United States Department of Justice, at a nonprofit fundraiser in California, and to a variety of civic groups and churches. All the while, I knew this was what I was supposed to be doing, but still didn't understand exactly what the future held for me in this journey to help others through sharing my story.

As I talk about sharing my story, I think it is important to note that each and every one of us has a story. There is value in telling our stories: mine and yours. You may be reluctant to share your story, but the day may come when you find an opportunity to do just that and you realize that in that moment, yours is the story that most needs to be told.

In 2014, I told my story at a business meeting of bankers. Whenever I finish a speech, I'm typically approached by some of the attendees with questions or comments, and this time was no exception. During my talk, I had mentioned having a bad credit record, because of the years of self-destruction I had caused in my adult life. One of the well-dressed bankers said he was interested in helping me resolve some of those issues, and gave me his business card. I said I'd be in touch, but I remember thinking he and I were from opposite sides of the road, with little in common.

After about six weeks of seeing his business card lying on my dresser, I decided to reach out to him. In an email, I said I didn't know if he'd remember me, but if he did and was still interested in helping me, I'd welcome the opportunity to meet. He did, and we planned to get together for lunch a few weeks later. Before the meeting, I printed out my credit information, sad as it was, and listed all my debts and delinquencies. When we met, he looked at the list and, much to my surprise, said it was a sixty- to ninety-day fix. The beauty, I learned, of messing up your credit at a young age, is that you don't have time to get into too much debt before they stop giving you more money!

Week after week, I'd show up at his office and give him money I had earned. He'd call my creditors and negotiate a deal to resolve the issue. Over time, and meeting regularly, he held me accountable, showed me love, and encouraged me through both his words and the time he invested in me. I really didn't know much about him beyond the fact that he was someone with the right expertise who just wanted to help me. We still have a strong relationship and I consider him one of my biggest fans and greatest supporters in believing in the power of my story.

Ironically, it turns out that we really aren't from different sides of the road, and he's continued to impact my life in ways neither of us would likely have envisioned.

Building A Plan

In my sobriety I realized there was life beyond abuse, and I wanted to help others. Other children and other adults to make their own transition from victim to survivor, and ultimately, to thrive. Of course, I had little in the way of resources, but I wasn't going to let that stop me. Even during my adolescence and young adult years as I faced many challenges, I had always been told I had confidence. The one thing I wanted to give to abused or neglected kids was that they could develop confidence in themselves, despite what had happened to them.

One of the things I remember most about my early meetings with my banker friend was sharing some of my ideas with him. He, in turn, told me that, as long as my plans were in my head, they were just dreams; they wouldn't become a plan until I wrote them down on paper. So I wrote out what I wanted to do. Living sober and telling my story were the first steps in the plan and then, about a year later, in 2016, the Keith Edmonds Foundation was formed. Its purpose is to regularly bring together kids who have been abused and neglected, and to help them develop self-confidence.

The next step was to create the kind of camp I both needed and wanted as a kid, but that didn't exist for me at the time. Camp Confidence became that camp and was something I was able to do through the Foundation. Camp Confidence would allow these children who've been abused and neglected to let go of their stress and do the things kids do best – just be kids.

One day, my banker friend asked me where I was going to get the kids for this camp I was talking about. I looked down as I was thinking about the answer and said, "The local juvenile judge." When I looked up, he had his phone out and was calling the local Juvenile Court Judge. A week later, I was in a meeting with the banker and the judge and Camp Confidence was becoming a reality.

During this time, I was driving for Uber, cleaning houses, and just really grinding to earn money to make this dream a reality. Because of this newfound relationship I had with the Judge, I was invited to attend and sit in his court any time it was in session. And that's how I became involved with the Wilson County Juvenile Justice System.

Chapter 13
Going Back To School

"A hundred years from now, it will not matter what my bank account was, the sort of house I lived in, or the kind of car I drove. But the world may be different because I was important in the life of a child."

~ Forest E. Witcraft

Not long after the Foundation was up and running, I was asked to be on a child abuse awareness panel, which included two survivors of child abuse, law enforcement personnel, Department of Children's Services caseworkers, and school staff members. The other survivor was a woman, and she told her story before it was my turn to talk. As I sat and listened to her share the horrors of the years of abuse she endured, I remember thinking to myself, "I have no idea how I'm going to follow this woman." The story of my face being held to an electric heater seemed insignificant, compared to what she had gone through.

When my turn came, I spoke of the abuse that led to my face being scarred, but more importantly, my message was that the abuse both she and I endured as children could not and should not continue to happen.

When the event was over, a woman who had been in the audience followed me out to my truck and said she wanted to have a meeting with me. She told me she worked for Wilson County Schools as the Coordinator of the Family Resource Center, which helps indigent families with children in local school system. We agreed to meet the following week.

When we met, Ann told me that the reason she followed me out to my truck that night was because

I didn't talk about myself as a victim. I didn't seem to wallow in what had happened to me or to have a victim mentality. In her work she deals with many families that have truly been through and are in tough times. Many truly are victims, and she tries to help them find ways out of their situations. She said that hearing me speak impacted her and she thought I needed to be involved with the school system.

Meeting Ann opened the door to that involvement. We met and talked for about an hour and discussed my desire to help hurting children, something we're both passionate about. She said I needed to get in front of the upper level leadership of the school system, so a few weeks later, I found myself in a meeting that Ann set up with the Director of Schools, and several other leaders in the school system. Irony would have it that we met in the building where I do a great deal of my work today. We met in a classroom at The Academy. Little did I know that the first time I walked in the doors of The Academy would be the first of many and the beginning of a work that I hope continues and has a lasting impact.

Of course, I knew who the Director of Schools was and what she did, but I really didn't know *her*. I didn't know she shared that same heart and passion for helping students as I did and as I do. So, a few weeks after our first meeting, I got the blessing of the school leadership to become involved in the school system. That meeting took place in January, 2017, and, since then, my involvement in both the juvenile court system and the Wilson County Schools has made for a beautiful relationship and opened many doors to work with children, especially at-risk teens in Wilson County.

After having the meeting with the Director and other school leaders, and getting their blessing to work in the system, it seemed fitting for me to start my work at the school where the meeting had been held. The Academy is the alternative school program in Wilson County. Things started out a bit slowly for me there, as it seemed to take some time to figure out how I could help, but today I'm very pleased with how well it's going.

The Academy

My situation in school was a little different than it is for the students at The Academy, but I still see myself in them every day when I'm there, in group settings, or just talking one-on-one with them. There's a negative connotation to any Alternative School, but that negativity usually comes from those outside the school who really know nothing about it. Lots of folks think of Alternative as the place for those "bad kids." I can tell you they're not bad kids, the majority are kids who have made bad choices and, as a result, are paying some consequences for those choices.

There's a distinct difference between bad kids and bad choices. What someone does as a teen doesn't have to dictate what he or she will do as an adult. Some will correct the behavior and learn from making bad choices. But some won't. Although the world they live in and the one I grew up in twenty years ago are different, some of the core problems are the same: abuse, neglect, DCS custody, substance abuse, etc. Those are unfortunately timeless, not generational.

Someone asked me recently how I feel about The Academy and I said, "I'm most happy when I'm there; I feel content and fulfilled." That was a bit eye opening for me to stop and put those feelings into words. I'm at The Academy five days a week, unless I have other obligations. Some days it feels like I'm just hanging out there. But when a kid passes me in the hall and says, "Hey, Mr. Keith, can we talk today?" I know I'm doing more than just hanging out.

I talked in the last chapter about my relationship with the Judge and the Juvenile Justice System in Wilson County. One of the things that happens when I am in court is that the Judge assigns kids community service hours, and often they are told to get with me about doing those, especially if they are already at or are going to The Academy . That means that I do a lot of community service! We pull weeds, we landscape, we paint, we clean, we do whatever needs to be done at the school, and we do it together. For many of them I am a father figure and a mentor. I get right in there with them and work beside them, I don't just supervise them! And this provides one of the best ways I have found to get a kid to open up to me.

I'm an adult who cares and who has made a conscious choice to become involved in their lives. The fact that they allow me to be a part of their lives is where my happiness comes from. There are three themes that consistently run through our conversations: decision making, problem solving, and conflict resolution. I emphasize these because I know these are things they face every day of their lives.

I realize I'm not the only person in their lives who's going to water the seeds, but while I'm with them, boy can I water! I connect with some, but not all. If I can change just one life in a positive way, then I'm content. Primarily, I hope I give them what I think they aren't getting at home, and that's stability, accountability, and a strong sense of hope that they can change their lives. I want them to understand that a bad decision does not dictate their lives.

One of the most poignant things that has happened while I have been working at The Academy, happened on a day when I was wiping down every surface in the building with one of the kids who was doing court-ordered community service.

It was that time of year when kids in schools get sick, and there was a lot of flu and strep going around. Over a box of bleach wipes, this student said, "Hey, Mr. Keith, do you know that you are the favorite at The Academy." We both laughed, and I said, "Well, you know, I've always wanted to be the favorite at the alternative school". After another round of laughs, I asked her, "What makes you say I am the favorite?" Her response is one I play back in my mind when I wonder if I am making a difference with these kids. She said, "Because you're our fan. You never give up on us, you push us to do better, and you spend time with us." That was a moment of validation for me, and one I will never forget. Her response touched my heart, and it also summed up everything I wanted as a kid, but rarely got.

If you really look at it, there are many kids who are abused and/or neglected who take their hurts and end up doing dumb things that get them into trouble – trouble at home, at school, and even with Juvenile Court. It goes back to something I say often and is a paraphrase of a saying I've read and use: that people who are hurting tend to hurt other people. For me, those two things went hand in hand, and I see that every day in the kids I am fortunate enough to work with in Juvenile Court and at The Academy.

Chapter 14
Unfinished Business

"When priorities are in place, one can more patiently tolerate unfinished business."

-Russell M. Nelson

Things were finally going my way. I was living sober and doing what I knew in my heart I was meant to do. I had found an amazing advocate to help me with my personal financial mess. I had met the Juvenile Judge and got started working with the court. I had met with the upper brass of the school system and had begun my work at the alternative school. The Foundation was off to a blazing start.

We were planning an event called *Shine the Light,* and it was going to be great. It was being planned for April, which is Child Abuse Awareness Month. We were going to help all these kids. We had invited the community and we were bringing awareness to child abuse. We were focusing on how to empower the community to be a part of the fight against child abuse, rather than just telling horrific stories of abuse. In other words, we were on a roll. I felt good, and was living the life that was unfolding before me. And then, in May 2017, I went back to Michigan, and it all threatened to unravel.

A friend of twenty years who was living in Michigan called me and asked if I'd come up there to help him move. He is a great friend and I had a truck, so I said, sure, I'll come and help. As we were driving from his old place to his new place with a load of his belongings in the back, we saw blue lights in my rear view mirror. For the first time in my life, those blue lights didn't cause me any fear. I pulled over, rolled down my window, and waited for the officer to approach. I was thinking, no big deal, right? Wrong!

The cop came up to the window and asked for my license and registration, which I gladly gave him. He went back to his car, and did the thing cops do when you get pulled over. He came back and said something I'll never forget: "Do you have any unfinished business in Eaton County?" I was a bit stunned, but told him I'd been in a car crash there seven years earlier. Apparently there was a warrant out for my arrest in Eaton County as a result of that accident. He said he was going to see if they wanted him to bring me in.

While he was back at his car, I looked at my buddy and told him we needed a plan to bail me out of jail. He didn't think I was serious, but I knew what was about to happen. I had been down this proverbial road before and I knew where I was headed when the officer returned. I gave him my keys and wallet, and we made a very quick plan for him to follow after the officer came back. Sure enough, in a matter of minutes, I was in handcuffs in the back of a police car, under arrest.

I couldn't believe where I found myself. I was five years sober and sitting on a bench, in jail, under arrest. I don't know why I was surprised, because actually I was right where statistics say I should have been. I have heard that statistically, two out of three victims of child abuse will end up in jail. Sitting on that bench, I thought about what I was building back home in Tennessee. I didn't want all of that to come crashing down because my past had caught up with me.

I hadn't even known there were any charges pending, because I didn't get arrested at the time of the accident, so I thought that was all just a part of the story of my past. But I still had some consequences of my actions to deal with. My buddy came and bailed me out, and the next day I headed back to Tennessee.

The day after I returned I went to see my banker friend. I went right away because I knew this was going to be one of those hard things and I wanted to get it out in the open and figure out how best to deal with it. I walked into his office, closed the door, and said, "I'm going to tell you something I never thought I'd have to tell you. I got arrested last weekend." After I explained it was for a charge from 2010, he assured me he'd walk along beside me in this new aspect of the journey.

I knew if I was convicted I'd have to spend time in jail, because it would be my second DUI conviction. My biggest fear was that all the work I had put into helping children and being involved in their lives would be null and void if I had to go away for six months. I was dealing with some of that "wreckage of the past" we talk about in the recovery community.

So I hired an attorney and went back to Michigan, yet again, for my first court date. They required a drug and alcohol evaluation, which was wonderful to do at almost five years of sobriety, because I could give real answers to all the questions. It's a totally different game when you can be completely honest. I couldn't have done it if I were still drinking. Although I was being honest, I still had an underlying concern about the consequences of jail time if I were convicted. I could imagine all I was building back in Tennessee crashing down around me.

The court dates went on for several months, and I was traveling to and from Michigan. I finally went in front of the judge and was given the opportunity to speak. For the first time, I wasn't an angry man before a judge. I told about my scars, the ones on the outside *and* the ones on the inside. I've already shared how I blew up in front of the last judge who had asked about the scars on my face, but the five-year sober version of me was different than the earlier version, and I was able to talk about it and share my story.

I told this judge about my recovery and working with at-risk, abused, and neglected children in middle Tennessee. By God's grace, the charges were reduced to reckless driving. When it was finished, I walked out of the courtroom, paid my fees, and drove back to Nashville.

This experience of being arrested again, after getting my life on track and being in a really good place, is very important in my story. It could have been my undoing, my unraveling. I could have picked up a drink and said "screw it" to everything that had been happening. I could have allowed the consequences of my past to put an end to the amazing future I was building in Tennessee. I want you to understand that I get it.

Our pasts are just that: the past. They are a part of the story, your story and mine, that we can't rewrite. I have found that if I try to hide those ugly parts of my past, they have a way of making themselves known. They sometimes rear their ugly heads and try to mess up everything happening in the now.

My hope for you is that as you read this, you understand that my life after getting sober and after getting things on track, hasn't been all rosy. And that yours probably won't either. After whatever, you can fill in the blank with the event or events that have changed you, and that maybe seemed to de-rail you, after that, you have a choice to make. I hope that by sharing my story and my choices that you find your own strength to get back up and get back on track when life, or your past life, kicks you in the teeth.

Chapter 15
A CODE Of Values

"Values are not a spur of the moment action. They are non-negotiable principles that guide our everyday lives. Your personal convictions, not those of others, determine how you live. "

~Harvey Mackay

If you've made it this far, then you understand that my life has not been easy. I've lived through some adversity. I've always heard that hindsight is 20/20, and I think after having lived my life to this point, and after having written much of it down for this book, I know that statement is true.

As I look back, I realize there have been four values that have influenced every part of my life, even in the darkest hours. Today, I lovingly refer to them as the CODE, and it is what I live by. At the end of this endeavor of writing down my story and sharing it in a very public and permanent way, my most earnest desire is that you, the person reading this book, find hope and meaning in my words. And that you can apply my CODE to your own life.

These are the traits, characteristics, whatever you want to call them, that have preserved my life to this point and, I have no doubt, will carry me on to whatever comes next. This is what the word CODE stands for in my life: *Courage*, *Optimism*, *Determination*, and *Encouragement*.

C – as in Courage

Courage is the ability to do something frightening. At least that's my definition of it. I believe I've always had courage inside me, I think we all do, but we often live without recognizing it. That courage has to be activated or triggered in some way. Sometimes we mistake courage for survival. There were many years, years you've read about in these pages, where all I did was try to live through whatever it was I was living through. I had to survive.

Sometimes in life there are places that you have to go, situations that you have to face, and challenges that seem unfair. This is not the extraordinary: this is the common, the ordinary. We all go through our own scary places, hard situations, and challenges. The question, at least for me, has always been, how am I going to make it through this? The hardest part is that there is no definitive answer, no certain way that is right, no road map or directions.

I have a great deal of respect for the rap artist, Eminem. His lyrics talk a lot about digging deep inside yourself to get past the fear. That's courage. It's almost like being fearless, or being afraid, and doing it anyway! In his song, *I'm Not Afraid,* there is a lyric that says, "I guess I had to go through that place to get to this one." How true for my life! Oh those many dark places! It took every one of them to get me here. And here is a good place!

Maybe courage is that feeling deep down inside, the place we sometimes have to really dig to find, where we know that we can make it through. The place where we know that there really isn't a choice. We understand that it won't be pleasurable or fun or easy; yet, we also know that there is no other choice.

There have been times in my life when I thought I would never be able to pull myself out of the depths of my addiction/alcoholism, and self-destruction, but I was always able to hear a little voice inside myself that said, "You can, you will, and you must. There is no other option." The voice inside me is that of 14 month old Keith.

I believe we each have that voice inside of us, but sometimes we allow the other voices to drown it out. When I think back through my school age years, I wonder how I made it, and especially how I made it with a smile on my face, most of the time. All I can say is that I know that little voice, however faint it was at times, was a thing called, Courage.

Initially, I became aware of my own courage when I told my story for the first time, standing in front of people, my Mom and Coach B among them, and describing what happened to me. It was the first time I acknowledged publicly that I was abused and that my scars were a result of that abuse. Maybe that is when I moved from victim to survivor.

I also know that walking into that first AA meeting took a great deal of courage. I wasn't court ordered to go to AA, I decided to go, but I didn't *want* to walk into that meeting. Once I got in there, I wanted to find I didn't belong. I found out just the opposite.

Today I see courage in the young people I work with, through both the Keith Edmonds Foundation and The Academy. Sometimes I see it, but they don't see it in themselves. As much as I wish I could, I know I can't find their courage for them, but I'll do all that's in my power to help them find it for themselves. I think it all starts with recognizing that there's a problem, an issue, or something that needs to change. Then courage comes in to go beyond recognizing and acknowledging the problem, to actually doing something about it. It takes a lot of honesty to be courageous.

—In Other Words—

*"Your time is limited, so don't waste it living some-
one else's life and don't let the noise of others' opin-
ions drown out your own inner voice. Most important, have the courage to follow your heart and
intuition. They somehow already know what you
truly want to become."*

~Steve Jobs

*"I learned that courage was not the absence of fear,
but the triumph over it. The brave man is not he
who does not feel afraid, but he who conquers that
fear."*

~Nelson Mandela

*"Life isn't smooth, but it's the bumps that help us
find out who we are. And it's handling the bumps
that give us courage."*

~Sarah Morgan

O – as in Optimism

I've been called a pessimist. I'm not. I've always thought of myself as a realist. I find optimism challenging. I don't even like people who are overly optimistic, you know, those bubbly souls who skip through life. No, that's not me! But I have found value in working on and becoming an optimist, I just happen to be one who doesn't necessarily skip!

Optimism is a choice – one hundred percent. It's a daily choice for all of us. I don't think of optimism as everything and every day being good, great, or grand. Rather, optimism is waking up and realizing I have another day on Planet Earth to make the best day possible. Life is always going to be a challenge. There'll always be days and situations that give you a reason to cry, to get angry, or throw up your hands and say, "I quit!" Optimism is about outlook.

There have been several times in my life where I have been beaten down by this world. It has felt like it just kept hitting, even after I was down. Life can be relentless at times. Storms come and they go. Tough times come and they go. But sometimes it feels as if the storms and tough times last forever. It is in those times that our perspective must change, from one of hopelessness to one of hope.

It reminds me of a Michigan winter. I have mentioned that several of the truly tragic events and vivid memories of my life have taken place during an especially cold, Michigan winter. The winters there seem to last about eight month and it feels like they will never end. But they do. They end. And when they end, there is a beauty in a Michigan summer sunset and a Michigan summer night that is like no other. If you ever get a chance to visit Michigan in the summer, be sure to take in the sunset, and enjoy the evening when it doesn't get dark until around 10:00 p.m. During a Michigan winter I have to remember that the season will pass, and that one day the bitter cold will turn to Michigan summer nights with picture perfect sunsets.

I look at each new challenge that I face today with the same confidence I have when I look at a Michigan winter. I know that something positive will come, even out of the challenges, good things will come. Are you looking? I know I am!

—In Other Words—

"One of the things I learned the hard way was that it doesn't pay to get discouraged. Keeping busy and making Optimism a way of life can restore faith in yourself."

~Lucille Ball

"Optimism is the faith that leads to achievement. Nothing can be done without hope and confidence."

~Helen Keller

"If you approach your work with optimism and a can-do spirit, your attitude, plus your aptitude, will determine your altitude."

~Harvey Mackay

D – as in Determination

I have to admit my love of the Rocky IV film. I love it because every time I watch it, I think to myself there's no way Rocky can beat the Russian. But every single time, Rocky beats him! Every time. Rocky is determination personified!

Determination is this: when everything is stacked against you, and there's absolutely no way you can win . . . determination says, Watch ME!

I believe we could all agree that life can be re-lentless. It can challenge us and make us want to give up, to say, "I'm done. I've had enough". But what makes us say, "I've had enough, and I am not going to let this beat me!" You been there? I know I have! This is where determination comes into play. When you have had enough of the beat downs and you aren't going to take it anymore, you have a choice. To let it, whatever it is, win; or to find your own de-termination to get up and get out of the mess "it" has created in your life.

How often in your life have you been told you couldn't do something? That happened a lot for me. Earlier in this book, you read about my getting into Central Michigan University. The odds were very much stacked against me, not only to get admitted, but even greater that I'd never graduate. I'd graduated from high school by going to summer school, zero hour, and night school, with a 1.7 GPA, and was ranked number seven *from the bottom,* in my class. I made the Bottom 10, not the Top 10! I even heard that all I'd do at CMU was fail. I needed to be challenged, and those words were a challenge for sure! I like showing people I can do what they think I cannot do!

Determination is required in order to make big, real, and lasting change. Maybe you're thinking about something you'd like to change in your own life; it's going to take determination to make it happen. I sometimes call it a firmness of purpose. Whatever you call it, determination is required for change to take place.

—In Other Words—

"You cannot keep determined people from success. If you place stumbling blocks in their way, they will use them for stepping-stones and climb to new heights."

~Mary Kay Ash

"Just don't give up trying to do what you really want to do. Where there's love and inspiration, I don't think you can go wrong."

~Ella Fitzgerald

"I determined never to stop until I had come to the end and achieved my purpose."

~David Livingstone

E – as in Encouragement

We all need encouragers in our lives, and they don't have to be limited to family members. Families are a blessing, no doubt, but not required. It doesn't take a sharing of DNA to encourage one another. Look around you. Think about the people in your life. I'm guessing you can name at least one person who encourages you. And if you find yourself lacking in encouragers, find some new people who can and will encourage you! And always know that I am in your corner, encouraging and cheering you on!

Encouragement can be a funny thing. Sometimes the voice of encouragement comes in the form of the voice of negativity. This relates back to my thoughts on *determination*. It's like when someone tells you that you can't do something, and you want to do it that much more just to show them. I've heard the voices of the haters, the naysayers, and I have thought, hold on, and buckle up, 'cause I am about to show you what I can do. I'm not talking about being pompous or boisterous. I'm talking about turning the negative into the positive.

When I was a kid, I remember hearing a country song by Johnny Cash, called, "A Boy Named Sue". The song is about a man who fathered a child but knew he wouldn't be around to raise the boy, so before he left, he named the boy Sue, which is traditionally a female name. The song goes on to explain that the father named the son that to make him tough, because he figured with a name like Sue, he would have to get tough or die!

Looking back on my own life, I know I had to get tough, or die. I think that many of the choices my mom made were for this same reason. She became a teen mom when I was born, and the mother of an abused child when I was burned. My life hasn't been easy, but neither has hers. Brenda did what she did to encourage me, even when sometimes it may have not felt that way.

I've been blessed to have a number of encouragers in my life. Because of them, I seek to be that to others, especially the young people I get to work with daily. Encouragement doesn't have to be loud and lively. Little bits of encouragement throughout the day can make big differences. I walked into the convenience store down the street from my home the other day, and someone held the door for me. The nice lady at the cash register said "Nice shirt. That color blue makes your eyes pop." I walked a little taller after that. It was a bit of encouragement as my day was getting started and it was nice, it felt nice. It's there if you're purposeful in listening for it and hearing it.

If you only hear discouragement, the voice of encouragement may get drowned out. "You'll never amount to anything." "You may as well give up now and stop wasting time." "You're worthless." I heard those a lot, certainly more than I'd like.

If those are the only voices you're hearing, stop listening! I hate it when any of our Academy kids tell me these are the things they hear from the people in their lives. No wonder they make bad choices! We all need to hear the voice of encouragement and part of that is to *be* an encourager. And please don't think you have to be in a place of authority to be an encourager.

Have you driven through a Chick-fil-a lately? Every employee is so polite. They smile. They say, "It's my pleasure to serve you." Are they being insincere? I don't know, but there's a consistent politeness and kindness I get when I go there, and it makes me want to keep going back!

Another aspect of encouragement is to recognize that people come and go in our lives. The voice of encouragement today may not be the same ones tomorrow. If we're blessed with having some constant voices of encouragement, then we are truly blessed. If I called Coach B today, his would still be a voice of encouragement. What a blessing he's been in my life! Don't miss the new voices while you yearn for the old ones. Listen and look for those people who encourage you. Embrace them, because you need them!

Take the negative voices and let them encourage you. Let them give you an extra push to say, "Watch me". Take the positive voices of encouragement and allow them to comfort you and push you to believe in yourself. And at the end of it all, be an encourager to those around you, because I am betting they need to hear it as much as you do.

—In Other Words—

"What kinds of words can we use to encourage others? Words that heal, words that help, and words from the heart."

~Nancy Parker Brummett

"Encouragement is not the responsibility of a gifted few; it is the privilege of every believer. Every Christian can and should be an encourager."

~Larry Crabb, Jr.

"Encouragement is food for the heart, and every heart is a hungry heart."

~Patrick Morley

The CODE

As I go through my life, I live by this CODE rather unconsciously at this point. It hasn't always been that way! I didn't wake up one morning sober, running this foundation, working with these kids, and writing this book. You have read the story and you know it didn't happen like that!! It's taken me some time and my path has been much the "broken road", as described in the lyrics from a country music song. But I'm here today because of the CODE.

My hope for you in all of this is that you find the *courage* I know is inside you, just waiting to be activated. Make every day the best it can possibly be, regardless of the wind and rain, because you have the *optimism* to understand that even a bad day can be a good day with the right attitude and outlook.

May you become like Rocky and beat the proverbial Russian in your life, _every time_, because you have the *determination* to do the work others say you can't do. Pay attention, acknowledge, and appreciate both the big and small *encouragers* who are in your life every day, and seek to be an *encourager* to others.

Epilogue
Setting The Prisoner Free

"I think the first step is to understand that for-giveness does not exonerate the perpetrator. For-giveness liberates the victim. It's a gift you give yourself."

— *T. D. Jakes*

Becoming a victim happens when someone does something to us or when something happens to us that is beyond our control. Becoming a survivor happens when we choose to do something for ourselves. Just getting through it or living through it doesn't make us survivors.

197

When we are still living in the loneliness, the anger, and the confusion, we are still living as victims. To become a survivor, *of anything*, requires time and circumstance. But the biggest thing that it requires is one of the hardest things for us humans. Becoming a survivor requires forgiveness.

There comes a time when you take a look at someone who has wronged you. Whether that person bullied you, told lies about you, stole something from you, or abused you, you ask yourself these questions: Why did this happen to me? What did I do to deserve this pain? Your initial thought is revenge: "I'm going to get even with that person." Then you think about resentment: "I can't stand that person. I *hate* that person! How could anyone do that to me?"

I went through all of those emotions over the man who abused me. To this day, I have never met him. Never found him. I wanted to. The day I met my biological father for the first time, I wasn't looking for him, I was looking for my abuser. I was looking for revenge. I never got it. And maybe that was part of the plan for my life. It would have served no good purpose for me to have found him. Not that day. Not ever. I don't even know if he is dead or alive. And today, it doesn't matter. I have forgiven him. Not for him. But for me.

There were times when I'd come home from school, go into my room where I was alone, and I'd cry and scream. I didn't understand why I had to go through what I was going through. Every time I thought of the man who abused me, I would ask myself, "Does he care that I have these scars? Does he care that he caused me so much pain and ridicule?" And every time, I'd come up with the same answer: No! This realization only led to more anger and more pain. But the day finally came when I reached a new realization. If I held on to this anger – this hate – the person I was hurting the most was me.

It wasn't until I was older that I came to another realization about my anger and resentment. It wasn't just my abuser I was angry with: it was also my mom. It wasn't just my abuser I needed to forgive. I also

needed to forgive my mom. I was angry with her because she had allowed us to be put into the situation
that resulted in my life being changed forever. I came
to understand that she was doing the best she knew
at the time. She was a teenage mother, just a kid trying to raise a kid. The abuse I suffered didn't just
change my life: it also changed hers. I have forgiven
my mom, and I appreciate her strength. I know her
love for me is unwavering.

As you near the end of this book you may be
thinking of the person who hurt you. We have all
been hurt by someone. Maybe it was a broken heart.
Maybe you don't carry outward scars, but it is hard
to live to adulthood without some scars on the inside.
If you are still holding onto the anger, resentment,
hatred, and the need for revenge, please trust me
when I say that you will never have a happy, peaceful, and content life until you find it within yourself
to forgive.

There are very few promises I can give you. But
the one I can is that if you let go of things from the

past that have caused you harm, *you will* find for-giveness. Forgiveness doesn't change the outcome of a situation, forgiveness doesn't excuse a person for his or her actions, but forgiveness does allow you to build a life you love. Forgiveness doesn't remove scars, but it does make life sweeter. Forgiveness isn't for the person that receives it: forgiveness is for the person who gives it. I love how the late author and seminary professor Lewis B. Smedes expressed this truth. He wrote: "To forgive is to set a prisoner free and discover that the prisoner was you.

And finally, I leave you with some words from one of my favorite musical artists, a fellow Michigander, and a brother in recovery:

"And to the rest of the world, God gave you the shoes that fit you, so put 'em on and wear 'em, and be yourself man, be proud of who you are. Even if it sounds corny,

Don't ever let no one tell you, you ain't beautiful."

-Marshall Mathers

CPSIA information can be obtained
at www.ICGtesting.com
Printed in the USA
LVHW021244040920
665076LV00016B/708